the Healing Power *of* Reiki

About the Author

Raven Keyes is a Reiki master, teacher, certified hypnotherapist, and guided meditation instructor. She was part of the original Complementary Alternative Medicine program at Columbia Presbyterian Hospital led by Dr. Mehmet Oz. In the world of professional sports, Raven has brought Reiki to athletes in the NFL and NBA. Featured in national magazines such as *Vogue* and *W*, she was named "Best Reiki Master in New York" by *New York Magazine* and was televised as "New Yorker of the Week" on NY-1 for providing volunteer Reiki services for eight and a half months after 9/11. Raven lives in New York City with her musician/composer husband, Michael Pestalozzi, and their dog, Murphy.

A Modern Master's Approach to Emotional, Spiritual & Physical Wellness

the Healing Power *of* Reiki

Foreword by Mehmet C. Oz, M.D.

RAVEN KEYES

Llewellyn Publications
Woodbury, Minnesota

FIRST EDITION
First Printing, 2012

Cover art: Fern leaf: iStockphoto.com/Paweł Burgiel
Cover design by Kevin R. Brown

Library of Congress Cataloging-in-Publication Data (Pending)
ISBN: 978-0-7387-3351-7

Llewellyn Publications
A Division of Llewellyn Worldwide Ltd.
2143 Wooddale Drive
Woodbury, MN 55125-2989
www.llewellyn.com

Printed in the United States of America

For:

my mother, Josephine T. Mazza Somers,

who graced me with her love

and

my father, Raymond G. Somers, Sr.,

who taught me to be brave

Dedicated to:

Michael Pestalozzi, thank you for playing the musical score for my life

and

John J. Keane, Jr., thank you for being my son

Contents

Acknowledgments

There are so many people, both living and on the other side of the veil, who have made this book possible. Relatives, friends, clients, and students alike have brought joy to my heart as I've walked along my life's path. I've been blessed to be in the presence of so many wonderful people who have been a part of my work, and they are reflected in this book, whether or not they are named. I send a big "thank you!" to each person who has graced my life; thank you for the part you have played in my story.

First and foremost, it was my family who shaped me into the person that I am. I thank my darling mother, who in her days on earth always told me I should write. She was my inspiration. My father gave me more things than I have words for. I'm glad to have grown up with my siblings, with whom I shared many fun times as we grew up together. My grandparents, aunts, uncles, and cousins from three generations influenced my deepest soul. And I thank my son for opening my heart when I became a young woman.

My love and gratitude goes to my husband, Michael Pestalozzi, for his endless patience while I spent almost every hour of the spring, summer, fall, and winter doing nothing but typing to create and then edit this book. Thank you, my darling, for being my constant support, and for gracing me with the safe haven of care you provided while I put my story into words.

For being incredible sources of inspiration to me, as the healing powers they are in the world, my gratitude and praise goes to Grete Fries, Stacey Lei Krauss, Elaine Egidio, Wendy Henry, Sandra Ingerman, Lady Olivia Robertson, Linda Taylor, Tom Cowan, and Lille O'Brien.

Thanks to Equinox Fitness for providing a home for my ever-unfolding Reiki-infused meditation classes. Kudos to the Equinox PR department for sending writers to experience my work and bring it to the attention of the greater world.

I would like to acknowledge the dedication of Lieutenant William Keegan, Jr., Operations Commander at the World Trade Center site after 9/11 and coauthor of *Closure: The Untold Story of the Ground Zero Recovery Mission*. Without his permission, I would never have been allowed to bring Reiki into the Port Authority Police Department's trailer and to the officers he commanded. Thank you, Lieutenant, and thank you to all those who served after 9/11, including Team Romeo and every single volunteer—from those who stood along the West Side Highway to cheer as the rescue and recovery workers went by, to the construction workers who came from far and wide to help out, and everyone in between.

I don't have words with which to express the special thanks that go to my therapist, Bernice Belth, and to Reiki master Thayer Burch for assisting in my healing after 9/11 by giving me a road back from the abyss of PTSD.

Thank you to Brian McCafferty! It was you who encouraged me more than ten years ago to write down my Reiki stories in manuscript form. You were the first person to believe I really had a book in me!

With love, I thank my friend, Signe Pike, author of *Faery Tale: One Woman's Search for Enchantment in a Modern World*, for insisting I restart this project and for bringing it to Yfat Reiss Gendell of Foundry Literary and Media. You two were the powerful midwives who helped birth a new way for the river of information to flow.

Props to my agent, Brandi Bowles, for seeing the potential in my book proposal and making sure it made its way into the right hands with the best publisher for my material.

Thanks to my editor, Amy Quale, and to everyone at Llewellyn who worked so hard on my book.

And to Angela Wix, who acquired my book for Llewellyn Worldwide Ltd. To you I express my undying gratitude, along with deepest respect for your brilliant skills as an editor. Thank you for guiding this project along so it can fly on wings to the life it was always meant to live…

FOREWORD

By Dr. Mehmet C. Oz

Susanna was a modern cardiac surgery patient. As an intelligent and motivated user of our health-care system, she had done her homework and visited my office ready to discuss all the subtle aspects of heart surgery. The conversation evolved from the nuances of mitral valve repair into a discussion of the responsibility that patients should bear in helping themselves recover after illness. Susanna was prepared; she had a nutrition game plan, a mind–body approach, and her own energy healer, Raven Keyes.

Susanna had asked me if her personal Reiki master could be present in the operating room to channel healing energy during the surgery. They had already established a very strong and long-lasting relationship and Raven's résumé was substantial. Yet, on the surface, bringing an energy practitioner to the operating room attacks the foundation of modern medicine, a field that seeks to measure objective benefits from every treatment.

My rationale in examining energy healing as a complement to allopathic medicine requires more space than is available in this brief foreword. In my devotion to save the lives of my patients through the powers of modern surgery and medicine, I am also intimately aware that survival is multilayered. Certainly New-Age physics has taught us that we can have two mutually exclusive hypotheses, like particle and wave theory for light transmission, that nevertheless share the truth in describing reality. Although difficult for the medical community at large to accept, an energy worker and a surgeon may be able to assist one another to ensure the "full recovery" of the patient. Organized medicine must help shoulder the responsibility to study these challenging new theories of healing. With this need in mind, my colleagues and I have supported the establishment of a Complementary Care Center at Columbia University and New York-Presbyterian Hospital to assist patients in dealing with the medical challenges before them.

A human life is more than just a physical unit, so understanding illness is often difficult. Unconventional healing techniques can offer promising results, although our ability to appropriately use these therapies is often limited. When a patient prepares for surgery, he or she may benefit from hypnotherapy, meditation, yoga, and energy healing (Reiki). These tools create a much different experience for the patient, who now feels more in control. Having a sense of power can be comforting to someone who is putting their life into the hands of others while they are under anesthesia.

My gift is surgery. Raven's gift is energy healing. I passionately focus my whole life and all my attention on performing perfect surgical procedures. Raven "listens" just as wholeheartedly to "hear" the patient's inner life needs. Although we cannot scientifically measure the impact of energy workers, I enjoyed watching the bond between Susanna and Raven help Susanna weather the challenges posed by heart surgery. If done correctly, surgically repairing or replacing a heart prolongs life and improves quality of life. These benefits are tangible and can be measured because they exist in a natural plane. By channeling energy and by providing that same patient with the freedom to address their fears on mental, emotional, and even spiritual levels, healers like Raven believe they can repair or replace inner issues so the patient can enjoy the future. Although scientific measurement of these benefits is not possible, I feel obliged to study her approach and impact. By challenging me to look more deeply into the labyrinth that leads to health, Raven is making me do a better job.

Raven was brave enough to enter the OR. She faced a medical procedure of extreme magnitude without the preparation one normally receives in medical or nursing school. What she brought with her was love for her client and her insights on energy medicine. During the procedure, Raven and I both supported and shared Susanna's desire to safely navigate through the waters of her most difficult challenge. With her team assembled, Susanna could rest. She could face her surgery, trusting in the knowledge that we were all there with and for her. And Raven had become my partner in the study of the heart.

—Mehmet C. Oz, MD
Columbia University
New York-Presbyterian Hospital
New York, New York

Introduction

My name is Raven Keyes, and I am a Reiki master.

For the better part of the past twenty years, I've been practicing Reiki, an ancient form of healing, while educating people about its uses in the modern world. I've seen Reiki heal pro athletes by reversing career-ending injuries. I've watched it help cancer patients undergoing chemotherapy. I've witnessed its powers to mend the abyss of heartbreak opened up by the loss of a loved one. Reiki is one of the most effective, accessible, and natural healing modalities around today, one that's being incorporated slowly into both hospitals and athletic programs across the country. Unfortunately, despite the beneficial emotional- and physical-healing impact that Reiki has, the majority of people walking the streets of our modern world have never heard of it. That's the very reason I'm writing this book.

In my many years as a practitioner, the work I've done with Reiki has taken place on large world stages: I was down at Ground Zero for several months after 9/11, administering Reiki to rescue and recovery workers as they struggled to clear the bodies and debris from the pit. I've gone into the operating room at New York-Presbyterian Hospital/Columbia University Medical Center with internationally known heart surgeon and TV host Dr. Oz to perform Reiki while he operated on a cardiac patient. And I've done Reiki for the football players of the NFL in their locker rooms next to the steel tubs they fill with ice for Sunday post-game body soaks (anything to avoid missing out on the rest of the season). Mostly, though, I share my practice with everyday folks who, consciously or not, need deep healing in their lives. This might be physical healing. Currently, I'm involved in a new integrative medicine project at New York Presbyterian Hospital/Columbia University Medical Center, where I treat the breast cancer patients of Dr. Sheldon Marc Feldman, Chief of Breast Surgery. This also might be emotional healing. Many clients come to me explaining that they feel stuck in their lives due to everyday things like the death of a loved one, a divorce, the loss of a job, the illness of a beloved child, or the strain of caring for an aging parent. In addition to my private practice, I teach Reiki and certify new Reiki masters. I believe I've seen every facet of what Reiki is and what it can do.

As I begin to share what I know about this amazing modality, it makes sense that I tell you a few things about my own personal road to Reiki. This is important, because I want you to understand that although I've worked on world stages, I come from simple beginnings. The facts of my life itself are a testament to Reiki and to its transformative power—my life is proof that once you surrender to the path that Reiki sets beneath your feet, amazing things begin to happen, whether you believe they will or not.

In my earliest memory, I'm about three years old, running across the backyard of our home, my chubby legs pumping beneath me. Around me the sunlight is making patterns through the leaves of the trees and my feet are pounding the earth fast, fast, fast! With the shady summer air coursing through me, through my lungs, I throw my head back and I laugh from a bottomless fount of joy, because I'm alive, alive, alive! I am bursting with energy, the energy of life itself—I feel it inside me, and all around me at the same time—I am joyously connected to *everything*!

This is my first recollection of experiencing what I later came to know as Reiki.

I grew up the eldest of what eventually became six children. My father worked in construction and my mom stayed home with us kids—my three sisters, two brothers, and me. Our little house was a tangle of limbs and constant activity. My grandmother lived next door in an apartment above the garage, and in the evenings she and my mother would cook together in the cozy kitchen, filling it with the smells of garlic, roasting meat, and earthy potatoes.

Growing up, I was expected to help my mother take care of my brothers and sisters; most of the time I didn't mind, even though I was just a kid myself. I loved my mom and was glad to be of help to her. But I always longed to be out in nature where things were quiet and peaceful. There, I could feel the energy of the earth beneath my feet, connect with the magic in the trees and the flowers, and breathe in the power of the seasons. Without having any words for it back then, I always could feel the loving energy in all things.

As a little girl, I was obsessed with fairy tales. I wandered the fields of Danbury, Connecticut imagining I was Maid Marian from *Robin Hood*, or fantasizing that King Arthur and the Knights of the Round Table were going to spring out from behind a hedge at any moment. I could revel in simple things, like the way the autumn leaves shocked red, orange, and golden yellow before drifting into a crisp carpet all around our house. Or the way the yellow stalks of corn poked through the snow in the shortened days of winter.

Those are the warmest memories, the ones I most like to revisit from childhood.

There is another set of memories, not so pleasant, that ended up affecting me in later life. These are the ones that resulted from a trauma I suffered as a very young child. The incidents of which I speak happened when I was less than five years old. It was an early Saturday morning in the fall when my sister Sharon and I were awakened ahead of everyone else, dressed up in our finest clothes, and told we were going "someplace special." This turned out to be our local hospital, where my sister and I were dropped off. No one let on that we were getting our tonsils out because our parents were told we would be too frightened by this news. Plus, believe it or not, at that time in America's medical history, it was thought that if you just dropped a kid off and left, their crying would stop quicker. What a world of misinformation that was! I can't begin to tell you how scared we were.

After having our clothes taken and being put into nightgowns, we were brought to a room in which we were placed into cribs with very high bars. We were sharing our room with a little girl who had been burned in a fire. This just added to the horror and our hearts broke for her, because she never stopped crying from the pain she was in. We were terrified and had no idea what would happen to us next. Before we knew it, my sister and I were strapped down on tables and taken into a hallway outside an operating room. We cried broken-heartedly, afraid we were going to be killed. I remember sobbing and calling out, "Goodbye, sister!" sure that we were now meeting our end. Masks emitting fumes of ether were placed over our faces as we sobbed. The next thing we knew, we were waking up back in our cribs to the screams from the burned little girl, with throats so sore we couldn't swallow or speak. These bad memories would all come back to haunt me later on in my Reiki life.

Jumping ahead, I was just a few months past my eighteenth birthday when I married, with a desire to savor life, away from the responsibilities of my birth family. I felt the pull to experience that aliveness I had felt at age three, running with the earth under my feet, moving as fast as I could. Now I was running toward the things that mattered most to me as a young woman: being in love and becoming a mother.

When my darling son John was born, I was so preoccupied with trying to raise him the right way that it never occurred to me to think about God, life after death, or spirituality. It wasn't until John was about three years old that I received my first spiritual knock on the door. I was putting him down for his afternoon nap when he looked at me quite frankly (for a three-year-old) and said, "Mommy, I want to tell you where I came from."

There was something in his tone that struck me as oddly serious. "Okay, John..." I waited, perched at the edge of his bed.

"Well," he began, his little blue eyes wide, "I was in the woods with my father. But it wasn't *this* father, it was *another* father. And we were chopping down trees." He stopped and looked at me carefully as though worried I might scold him.

"John," I reassured him with a smile, "it's okay; you can tell me anything you want."

"Well, what happened next was that one of the trees fell on me! And my father picked me up, and he took me to my bed. And the doctor came. And the doctor kept trying to get me to open up my eyes. But I *couldn't* open my eyes! And the next time that I *did* open my eyes, I was with you."

I sat there stunned. Was my three-year-old son talking to me about *reincarnation*?

With John's proclamation, for the first time as an adult, I began wondering what might lie beyond the veil of our everyday existence. I didn't go to church much as a kid; my spiritual education consisted of learning "Now I Lay Me Down to Sleep," which was dutifully taught to me by my grandmother. Now that I was twenty-three, my son had opened a door of perception for me that was the beginning of my true path to Reiki, although I surely didn't know it at the time.

I'll skip over the years until John was a young man. By then, that initial awakening he had sparked in me became my inspiration to study Buddhism, where I became proficient at meditation and chanting. On the advice of a friend, I decided to add the study of channeling to the mix. The teacher discussed how he believed we were all born with spirit guides who had volunteered to accompany us throughout our lifetimes. According to the teacher, they do this for different reasons. Some volunteered to help us so that they could grow and learn themselves; others might be a relative with a strong emotional bond; some might have a connection to us from a previous lifetime. Then, of course, he explained there were the angels, here to help us find our way during our time on earth.

I sat there trying to absorb everything as he ran through the exercise at hand: learning how to get in touch with our spirit guides through a guided meditation. Aha! Meditation. *This*, I knew. I closed my eyes, allowing his soft voice to guide me into a deep state of relaxation.

I saw myself standing in the center of a circle, surrounded by six or seven human forms, their faces lost behind a milky white mist. Soon, a figure before me came into focus, and I was surprised to see it was a Native American man. Tall, with a strong build and disarmingly keen eyes, his face creased with wrinkles. His midnight-black hair was decorated with gray-white feathers, and golden earrings adorned his ears. I couldn't help but wonder why on earth—after everything white people had done to destroy their culture—a Native American man would be my guide? Nonetheless, I decided to play along, asking him if he'd tell me his name, as our teacher had insisted we do. His smile seemed to radiate as he answered quite openly. *My name is Little Raven.*

And what is your purpose? I asked him as I'd been instructed to do.

I am always right in front of you, guiding your path. I make the way for you. He held my gaze a moment before turning and sinking back into the mist.

When we came out of the meditation, I dutifully wrote down my experience, feeling like I'd accomplished my task. But I felt strange about it—I thought I must have some creative imagination, dreaming up a Native American spirit who wanted to be my personal guide. There was a part of me that felt like this was hilarious, imagining this guide watching me all the time. *Little Raven must really enjoy watching me when I eat pizza*, I thought. *I bet he gets a real kick out of seeing me put on eyeliner.* But as I took the subway home that night, the man's face continued to flash across my mind so vividly, I could still recall the smallest details: the creasing of his skin, the strands of silver hair threaded through the long black curtain of hair he wore pulled back.

A few weeks later, a friend came over for dinner and pressed a copy of a book into my hands, *Bury My Heart at Wounded Knee: An Indian History of the American West* by Dee Brown.[1] "You must read it," she said encouragingly. "I know you'll be moved by this."

Despite her endorsement, it sat on my shelf for a long while. I knew the importance of the book, but I also knew it was an absolutely heartbreaking story, one I wasn't sure I was prepared to read. Finally, on a whim one morning, I tossed it into my gym bag. I was on the Stairmaster when I flipped it open to a random page, only to find a shockingly familiar face looking back at me.

I nearly fell off the machine.

Regaining my balance, I blinked a few times just to make certain. There was no mistaking the high broad cheekbones, squared jaw, and deeply lined face, but it was the eyes that clinched it. My heart raced as my fingers traced the caption under the picture.

Little Raven.

As I read on, I discovered he was chief of the Arapaho Native Americans in the Colorado area when the white men came. Despite seeing countless women, children, allies, and great chieftains murdered in the land struggles of the 1800s, he was a tireless campaigner for peace and the safety of his people.

The exterior world had just verified what I had really already known deep down in my soul. This was a sign that showed up in time and space to let me know that Little Raven really was my guide. I've learned since then that this is how it always works. We are given insight into something during an inspired moment that will come to be revealed as truth by showing up with some sort of confirmation in the "tick-tock," or earthly, world.

With Little Raven's appearance, I was becoming consciously aware of a spiritual world hidden behind the one I usually dealt with. I began to wake up in the middle of the night, experiencing the strangest feeling that everything was about to change for me, that something new was coming. I somehow seemed to know that my past had prepared me for what my life was becoming. I thought about Little Raven all the time. But the thing that led me to ask more searching questions about him was the fact that more and more blackbirds kept showing up everywhere I went. It was those birds that got me to meditate in an attempt to contact Little Raven to ask him what all these things meant.

Sitting cross-legged on the living room couch, I allowed myself to drift into relaxation. I let my imagination take me where it wanted to lead, until I found Little Raven in a small clearing in the woods. He seemed to be glowing from within. He sat down across from me and looked directly into my eyes. It felt like he had been waiting for me. Before I even had the chance to ask a question, I was shocked when he said,

The blackbirds have been messengers from me. They fly between worlds and have been trying to bring you an understanding of who you are. I want you to know that I hereby give you explicit instruction and permission to use my name, "Raven." As the protector of the new path you will embark upon, I give you this name to use as your own as you walk into a whole new world.

I had no idea what this "path" and "whole new world" business could possibly be about, and I surely felt more than a little weird about taking his name, but all I could think of to do at the time was say, *Thank you.* He then began to glow even brighter from within his body. He held up his palms toward me, almost like a blessing, and simply disappeared. In the next moment, my awareness shot me back to my living room, where I found myself in tears. I felt so loved!

Following this communication with Little Raven, I heard the word "Reiki" for the first time. It happened after the very next channeling class I attended. As I was gathering my things together to leave for home, I overheard two of my fellow students discussing some sort of training to become Reiki masters. The hairs stood up on the back of my neck and I could hear Little Raven's voice inside my head saying "the new path."

"Excuse me," I smiled, nudging my way into the conversation. "I couldn't help but overhear... what's a Reiki?"

They glanced at each other and back at me, and then they just walked away.

I felt my cheeks flame in embarrassment—had I said something wrong?

Feeling shamed, I left it alone, figuring if this was how budding Reiki masters treated people, I didn't want any part of it anyway.

But our purpose in life has a way of finding us, even when we think we've dismissed it for good. The next afternoon, my husband Michael and I were having our usual weekly Yoga class with our teacher when she announced that, as an extra treat, she was going to give us a little Reiki during our postures, because she'd just received her certification. As she placed her hands gently on my back, I instantly felt a warmth flow into my body. My mood changed. Suddenly I felt lighter, happier, hopeful, calm, and strong—all typical responses to people's first encounters with Reiki. I was hooked! I wanted to know *everything* there was to know about Reiki. As soon as I could, I completed my training and was ready to begin treating clients.

I never could have imagined back then what this "whole new world" was about to become! As soon as I completed the training to become a Reiki master, without my trying to do anything, circumstances aligned themselves that resulted in my becoming employed by

Equinox Fitness. Lovingly known by all its members, trainers, and instructors as simply "Equinox," this company is a high-end national health-club chain with facilities in major cities throughout the United States. The next thing I knew, because Equinox has an amazing PR department, I was giving Reiki sessions in the Equinox spa to editors and writers from magazines like *Vogue* and *W.* Before I knew it, I was pronounced "Best Reiki Master" in New York by *New York Magazine* in their "Best of New York" issue! Through these magazine stories, word about Reiki started getting out into the world at large. By now I was also studying energy meditation with Reiki Master Lille O'Brien at her Expansion School of Higher Awareness, a fact known by my manager at Equinox. This led to my being asked to teach meditation classes, spiced with Reiki, at several of the Equinox clubs. These classes have continued to this day, bringing ever-expanding numbers of people into personal awareness about Reiki.

The events that unfolded in my life without my trying are indicative of what Reiki can do for anyone when the decision is made to follow the magical road Reiki sets before your feet. I would like to suggest that we are all born with our gifts and destiny encoded within us. Just like the seed of a tree blown on the wind already contains the entire tree it will become, so do we all have greatness inside, and Reiki will bring that greatness out in spades!

There are many books out there that discuss Reiki in a way that's tailored to people who are already familiar with it or to people who want to become practitioners. However, there are few books that share true human experiences with Reiki. After all these years of witnessing the transformative effect that Reiki can have, I decided that if sharing my personal stories—the patients, the healing, the stories of human triumph over hurt, and how it changed me—can help people better understand Reiki and the tremendous power it has to heal, then I have a responsibility to do so.

Reiki is a tactile art; masters are dealing with energy all the time in healing, and energy is often understood through how it makes us feel. So it's only natural that during sessions we have to listen to our feelings. I've included some exercises to help you get tuned in to the energetic forces that surround us all the time, so you can see what I mean.

Whether you are new to energy work and curious about Reiki or you are wondering if a career as a Reiki practitioner might be a good fit, what I present here will give you a bird's-eye view into what Reiki is and what it does. I will tell you things I think are important for you to know, introduce you to my clients, share helpful information along the way, and let you look through my eyes to see what a Reiki master does. I believe that observing my clients with their various conditions and circumstances and witnessing just how much Reiki helped them will assist you in making an informed decision about what "energy medicine," so named by Dr. Mehmet C. Oz, really is. Whatever you decide to do with the information I share, it's important to know that you cannot make a mistake! Reiki is intelligent energy; it automatically goes to where it is needed. The only thing required is that you always have the intention of allowing healing to happen. You do not control what comes, you only surrender to what Reiki already knows how to do.

Most of all, the willingness to try something new is what I hope you'll take away from this book. Perhaps you'll be interested to find out what Reiki might be able to do for you, or how it might fit into your life. Over the course of my book, I'll explain what Reiki is and what other things might come into your life because of it. You'll meet people with whom I've shared Reiki, which will give you the chance to see different types of issues that Reiki can heal. Finally, I provide helpful meditations that will enhance and clarify the different topics in Reiki, giving you a well-rounded understanding of the many elements of Reiki.

A few housekeeping notes concerning the meditations in this book:

- If you've never done meditation before, don't worry. Just follow along and use your ability to "pretend" as you go through the steps. Pretending frees you up to follow along without putting pressure on yourself.

- It's important for you to respect your own uniqueness. Allow yourself to have the experiences that await you in the way that's unique to you. It is not necessary to "see" things during meditation unless you are already a visual person. All the ways of perceiving your inner world are powerful and perfect, so just let yourself have these experiences in whatever way they come, whether it's through seeing, hearing, sensing, feeling, or just knowing something. Honoring what feels easy and natural to you is the most important key to experiencing the truth inherent in the meditation. By just trusting yourself and your own way of knowing, the various meditations and experiences I share cannot help but connect you to the beautiful energies as we move along.
- To enhance the meditation experience, you can record them and listen back to do them; read along, squinting your eyes open as you go to each new direction; or have a friend read them to you.

I now want to invite you to step into my world. I have some remarkable stories to share with you about the different areas where disease can enter: body, mind, emotions, and spirit. Don't worry if you're not sure how you feel about Reiki as we get started. As renowned Reiki master, teacher, author, and publisher of *Reiki News*, William Lee Rand, says, "Reiki isn't based on the need to believe in it in order for it to work ... To receive benefit, all that's necessary is to be willing to receive a session."[2]

Because it's so helpful for you to feel the healing power of energy firsthand, here's a meditation for that purpose.

Guided Meditation: The Energy of Golden Light

Part One: Breathing Practice

This meditation can be done either sitting or lying down. Get comfortable, with your spine straight. Close your eyes; notice, as you breathe in and out, how the air passes through your nose and watch as the air goes into your lungs. If your mind sends up thoughts, think to yourself, *I wonder what my next thought will be.* This will usually still the mind, but if you are still thinking, try to simply watch your thoughts as if they are clouds passing across the sky. Begin breathing in to the count of four, hold for four counts, and exhale for eight counts. Count as fast or as slow as is comfortable for you.

Do this four-four-eight breathing pattern for ten rounds, marking the completion of each round by counting on your fingers as you complete each exhalation. Once you count out ten rounds, let your breathing return back to normal.

Part Two: Accessing Golden Light

Now imagine a beautiful, golden, sparkling light beginning to form around your head and upper body. It can look as bright as early morning or as buttery and warming as late afternoon sunshine. Allow this glittering golden light to grow in size to surround you. The sparkles held within this light are the energies of everything positive: love, compassion, forgiveness, kindness, wholeness, tenderness, and every other wonderful thing you can think of.

Let the golden light continue to expand and extend outward, growing in size, flooding that space around you, your aura, with beautiful light. No physical object can interfere with this expansion—not walls, floors, objects, or other people. Your aura, six feet in all directions around you, is your very own unique and specific vibration. Allow that space to fill up with the light.

Now, as you breathe in, the golden light around you is traveling on the oxygen and enters your body. The light-filled oxygen fills your lungs as you breathe. The energy of golden light travels through your bloodstream, bringing blessings to every nook and cranny of your body—

soothing you, nurturing you, and raising your vibration with every breath that you take.

Notice how you feel inside as you continue to breathe in the golden light. You are whole. You are nurtured from the inside out. The golden light is the energy of living consciousness, energy full of blessings, just for you. Allow yourself to be at peace. Envision yourself glowing and vibrant. Feel inside yourself as you breathe. Know that in this very moment, you are doing everything you can to bring glorious perfection into your life. Experience yourself as happy and peaceful.

And so you are.

Stay with this for as long as you feel comfortable, and when you are ready, open your eyes and return your awareness to your physical reality.

Pursue some path, however narrow and crooked,
in which you can walk with love and reverence.
—*Henry David Thoreau*[3]

CHAPTER 1

What Reiki Is (and What Sometimes Comes with It)

To begin, it helps to have a few simple explanations to get started. First of all, Reiki is a form of gentle energy transmission administered through the hands of a practitioner. It is shared by softly touching the client's body, or by holding the hands just over the body, in a series of hand positions. It can also be administered remotely. (I will discuss these techniques in greater detail later in this chapter.)

Reiki is a healing practice with roots older than any written record. Placing our hands on our bodies is a natural response to injury, if you think about it. What's the first thing you do when you bang your shin or cut your finger? It's a natural reaction for your hands to go to or grab the point of injury instantly, instinctively.

Pronounced *ray-key*, this natural type of energy was discovered and put forth as a method for healing in Japan by Dr. Mikao Usui in the early 1900s. It is the energy of pure, unconditional love. In fact, the most profound description of it would be "love from the universe, shared through the hands." In Japanese, *rei* means spirit, divine, supernatural, or miraculous. *Ki* means breath, force, energy, or intention. This makes Reiki many things: divine breath, miraculous energy, supernatural intention, or spirit force. In 1937, Mrs. Hawayo Takata brought the Reiki method to Hawaii after studying it in Japan. Since then, it has spread throughout the United States and Europe. Today the term "Reiki" has come to mean universal life-force energy.

My years of practice have taught me a simple truth: Reiki is pure, unconditional love. It's that mystical "something" that enlivens our cells and holds the stars in place in the heavens. It's the creative force that humans have given so many names to in our world: God, Goddess, All That Is, etc. I think of it as a loving power that heals. Reiki restores balance; in a balanced state, self-healing naturally occurs. One of the things I like best about Reiki is that it doesn't matter who you are or what your leanings may or may not be; whether you're Christian, Buddhist, Jewish, Muslim, atheist, or even if you have no idea what you believe, anybody can connect with Reiki. All you have to do is just lie back and relax in order to receive its astounding benefits.

If you were to come to me for a Reiki session, you'd arrive at my office to find a soothing atmosphere of soft music and the scent of lavender. The lights would be dimmed to allow you the opportunity to unwind a bit from the outside world and to disconnect from whatever your day had thus far been. I'd explain my intention for the session: to channel Reiki's healing power to your body, mind, emotions, and inner spirit. Once you were comfortable, you'd lie down fully clothed on a massage table, and I'd ask you to relax, close your eyes, and just ... be. To begin treatment, I'd rest my hands softly on the midsection of your body. Coming through my hands you may feel warmth or a pulsing that is gentle and calming. That's because there is actually energy coming through my hands.

How?

Well, a Reiki practitioner is trained to access the loving energy that is all around us—in the cosmos, the atmosphere, and the world—in order to foster healing. It's not farfetched at all to consider we can learn how to draw in energy. In fact, it's the first law of thermodynamics; science has taught us that energy is in everything, down to the very matter that composes our bodies, and that it cannot be created or destroyed.[4] Instead, energy moves from one thing to another. From one being to another. For those who have felt Reiki's gentle, soothing warmth moving through them, and for those who have seen the power of Reiki transform their lives for the better, there is little doubt about what it can do.

You might ask: because this energy is inside everything and everyone, why would Reiki even need to be administered? That's a great question! To answer, I find that in today's world, people get energetically depleted and unbalanced from stress, bad relationships, family obligations, bad breakups, loss of a loved one, trauma, war, and don't even get me started on pollution. The list of what depletes and unbalances us goes on and on. Being depleted and out of balance leads to illness. A Reiki practitioner restores lost energy, allowing balance, harmony, and inner calmness to reestablish within. Reiki can even reverse physical ailments and injuries, as you will read about as we go along.

In my experience, the most important information that Dr. Usui passed on to us is that we don't need to know anatomy, or causes of disease, or anything else medical in order to do this kind of healing work. We are enabled to transmit the energy to heal by receiving the Reiki attunements from a master. These attunements clear a pathway within us, a path inside our bodies that allows the Reiki to flow into us at will. In our training, we learn to be like an empty glass in order to fill up with the pure light of Reiki, and then we pass it on. We are never drained; we are always full, no matter how many sessions we might be called upon to give. Reiki masters are vessels who receive the highest, purest level of universal energy that we then share in two distinct ways: with our clients for their healing, and with our students to awaken their abilities to channel Reiki themselves. In other words, by filling up with Reiki myself, I can work with my clients, or awaken within my budding Reiki students the ability to use Reiki in service to themselves and others.

I want to make it clear that a Reiki practitioner does not heal anyone—not ever. It's the Reiki itself that is responsible for any and all effects that result from what we as practitioners transmit. We are the vessels that allow this energy to fill us up and then flow out of our hands into our clients. A client under the care of a Reiki practitioner can then freely use the energy transferred to them to allow healing to naturally occur. In other words, a Reiki practitioner provides the energy with which clients balance and heal themselves.

This issue of self-healing through the power of Reiki leads us to the practicum that was eventually taught by Dr. Usui. After Dr. Usui discovered and began practicing Reiki, he spent a lot of time in the ghetto or Beggar's Quarters of Kyoto, Japan at the turn of the century. His goal was to use the magical practice to help impoverished citizens not only to heal from sickness, but also to take an active role in society. But it was through this very work with the struggling population that he came to understand more about the circumstances necessary for Reiki to be effective. You see, as time went by, Dr. Usui became aware of the fact that many of the people he was treating were not taking responsibility for their lives at all. They were depending on him to do everything for them. This created an imbalance, and realizing this flaw led Dr. Usui to a new discovery he made while in deep meditation—a discovery that changed the way in which he dealt with those who came to him for help.

First, he realized for Reiki to be effective, the recipient must have a desire for change and healing to occur. Second, if the help of another was involved in creating that healing or change, there must be an equal exchange of energy. By giving away healings, he had further impressed the beggar pattern in many of them. More than that, he saw that in order to maintain a sense of balance, as well as a sense of respect for the services he offered, people needed to give back for what they received. This can be a monetary payment, an exchange or barter, or a gift of whatever means that person might wish to give. Third, and of equal importance, the intended recipient must give their permission and allow themselves to be healed.

Reiki practitioners today still practice Reiki based on these principles. When a client is relaxed on the table, the Reiki practitioner silently sends out to that person's inner spirit a very specific question. We don't ask the client out loud, we ask their soul, or spirit. "Do I have your permission to give you Reiki?" All practitioners have their own symbol or signal for yes or no. For me, I typically see a green or a red light, like a traffic light. It's vital to have the permission of your client's spirit; otherwise, you're healing against their will, and this is not right. None of us has the right to treat someone whose spirit has a different agenda.

Trying to describe Reiki is like trying to describe love, but to give you a better idea of what it is, imagine there was a magical type of Band-Aid that could grow and stretch in size to treat any kind of wound, whether you'd fallen and scraped your knee or ended up in a head-on collision. Reiki is intelligent energy, and it can address anything, from a cut knee to a broken leg, cancer, depression, or even grief. In recent years, Reiki has been scientifically proven in medical and alternative health-care studies to reduce pain, increase memory, and help people heal faster than patients who did not receive Reiki treatments.

And perhaps Reiki's effects aren't so surprising when we consider our body's miraculous ability to self-heal. In recent years, shocking scientific findings in placebo research have been featured everywhere from the *Boston Globe* to National Public Radio. As Margaret Talbot wrote in a 2000 article in the *New York Times*, entitled

"The Placebo Prescription": "The truth is that the placebo effect is huge—anywhere between 35 and 75 percent of patients benefit from taking a dummy pill in studies of new drugs ..."[5]

In everything from depression to chronic arthritis to Parkinson's disease, the power of placebo—or really, the power of the human mind—has become so well accepted that even while researchers remain befuddled as to how and why placebos work, the effectiveness of all new medications is measured against the standards of placebo success. Though I certainly don't believe that Reiki acts as a placebo, the research into this human phenomenon is a clear testament to our mind–body connection, not to mention a clear demonstrator of just how little we understand about self-healing.

On September 15, 2008, the American Hospital Association put out a press release entitled "Latest Survey Shows More Hospitals Offering Complementary and Alternative Medicine Services," based on a survey conducted by their Health Forum. The Health Forum found that more than 37 percent of responding hospitals offered alternative medicine therapies in addition to their standard medical treatments.[6]

Now is the time that Reiki needs to be made accessible to everybody; it can help prevent illness before it sets in. Not everyone who comes to me is sick or suffering in any way. Some of my regular clients come for Reiki as a way to calm down, because it induces deep relaxation, even bliss. Many people fall asleep on the table, which is a natural healing practice the body already knows that is often induced by Reiki. Some clients experience being "off in another place," a place that is not quite sleep, but just as restful. No matter what, Reiki can only be used for the good and therefore is always an excellent way to take care of oneself. When stress is relieved, good health is nurtured and supported.

As stated previously, Reiki can be administered in person or via "distance" sessions. Regarding in-person sessions, practitioners have their own preference as to whether they share Reiki through the use of touch or with their hands held above the body of their clients. There's no difference in the effectiveness; it's a matter of how the practitioner prefers to work. Because I feel we don't have enough nonsexual human touch to soothe us in our lives, I prefer to place my hands directly onto the body, except, of course, on private parts, which is where I use the hands-over-the-body technique.

Some Reiki is administered with the practitioner and client in different locations. Commonly referred to as "distance healing," it is just as effective as an in-person session. When performing a distance healing, the Reiki practitioner uses a special technique that makes it possible to conduct the session with the spirit of the client rather than with their physical body. Because this knowledge is shared only when a student reaches the second level of training, I am not at liberty to divulge exactly how it works. What I can say is that, for the practitioner, there is a certain kind of purity to the experience. Some of my colleagues and students focus on the distance healing type of practice almost exclusively. Although I personally prefer to work in person, I have had many profound experiences giving sessions of the remote variety. You'll see what I mean as you read the distance healing sessions I have scattered throughout the book.

In some cases, working remotely is the only option. There's an uncluttered feeling that prevails with the spirit away from the personality and ego housed in the body. In these circumstances, I can always get a true read very quickly on what the client's situation is and what their spirit is gaining from the session. I seem to know right away if issues are physical, emotional, mental, or spiritual, even if I don't have a personal connection with the person. Though Reiki is intelligent energy that knows what needs to be done, in order to stay out of its way, it helps for the human part of the practitioner to hold the intention to facilitate healing, no matter what that might look like. Healing doesn't always mean a cure. A decision to cure comes from the ego, which must be left out of Reiki altogether. In some cases, the healing a person truly needs might be an easing through the dying process.

Another amazing aspect of distance healing is that you can provide a Reiki session to the spirit of someone who has died. As you will see, this type of remote healing is very soothing, not just to the person who has passed on, but also to the ones left behind, if the practitioner has the opportunity to share what transpired with the family.

In today's world, Reiki is generally taught in three levels, with attunements being administered by the Reiki master for each one. Reiki I is the foundation of the Reiki practice and teaches how to give Reiki to oneself, as well as the knowledge of how to use hand positions on another person. Reiki II expands on that foundation, teaching symbols to use during sessions and the procedures to follow for distance treatments. Reiki III, or Master Level, passes on knowledge of the master symbol and how to use it in order to heal the spiritual body. There is another level for those who wish to teach Reiki called the Reiki Master Teacher Level, in which one learns how to teach Reiki and how to pass on the attunements that go along with each level.

A Reiki practitioner is one who has gone through Reiki Levels I and II, and can practice Reiki on clients. A Reiki master, however, has gone through all the levels of training and perfected their craft. A master's ability to heal the spiritual body is very important, especially in cases where traumatic events have been experienced. When trauma is an issue, knowing how to bring healing to the spiritual body becomes of paramount importance. Although this is not part of allopathic medicine, the understanding of spiritual illness and ways to cure it have been known by shamans throughout history.

The attunements a practitioner receives are extremely important. The attunements (given by a Reiki master) develop the openings that allow the budding practitioner to become a vessel—that empty glass that can fill with Reiki and then transmit it to oneself or to a client through the hand positions learned in Reiki I.

You will find that it will eventually become necessary to connect with a living, breathing Reiki practitioner or master if you wish to experience a traditional session, or a Reiki master if you wish to study Reiki. Although you may read about Reiki in a book, the true knowledge of how to practice Reiki must come from a Reiki master who has been taught by another master how to pass on the attunements necessary to access Reiki. It's also important to know that in Reiki there is no hierarchy spiritually, i.e., a Reiki master is not considered to be more important than anyone else. The authoritative title of the Reiki "master" serves only to indicate the knowledge held and the abilities to transmit. The Reiki master is responsible for respecting the value in every Reiki practitioner and client, guiding them to recognize their own unique beauty and gifts.

An important aspect of what Reiki does for the person studying it is: you are never alone when you do Reiki. Reiki practitioners are the "receivers" of Reiki, much like a radio or TV that converts received information into sound and picture. When we have the intention of sharing Reiki, the energy of this divine love is transmitted to each of us by a member of a spiritual order in another dimension called *Reiki masters in spirit.* Reiki masters in spirit are spirit guides who have volunteered to help us administer the unconditional, loving energy that is Reiki healing. An easy way to understand this is perhaps to compare them to angels that work on behalf of divinity. In fact, my Reiki master in spirit is an angel, but not all of them present themselves as such. It's not because I picked the angel as my guide—that's who showed up when I went through the process to find out who was going to be working with me in my Reiki practice. You can find your own Reiki guide by using meditation.

If you decide to become a practitioner yourself, the agreed-upon recommendation is to have your training in the physical presence of the Reiki master you choose. There are websites that offer distance Reiki attunements as well as distance group attunements.[7] In conversation with William Lee Rand, we both agreed that Reiki attunements and training should be done in person. Rand pointed out that all respected Reiki master teachers he knows agree that in-person attunements are necessary. On a practical level, it's very difficult to learn Reiki from a distance. It's important to be in the physical presence of the person who is training you so they can observe and help you to make any necessary adjustments, or answer any questions that might come up for you. I have included in the Further Reading section at the end of the book a link to an article written by Rand on this subject, along with a link to approved Reiki teachers in Rand's organization.

If you are intending to connect with a Reiki master in your town or neighborhood, take time to research. You can ask friends for recommendations, check in with your local health-food store or vitamin shop, or look online. Make sure to investigate the practitioner's qualifications. Prices for training (and for treatments) vary greatly, and price doesn't always equate with quality. If at all possible, I recommend directly contacting anyone with whom you are considering studying Reiki and having a conversation to make sure you feel comfortable. You also want to make sure in advance that, for the price you will pay at each level, you will receive:

- complete training,
- proper attunements, and
- a certificate of completion.

You will also need a manual of some kind. If your teacher does not have their own, be sure they are able to recommend one that you can acquire.

Once Reiki comes into your life, your life will begin to flourish in ways you never anticipated. The spiritual code imprinted within you endlessly unfolds, and the flower of life itself reveals its true beauty to your heart.

As this happens, a path naturally forms beneath your feet: a path to new information and ways of being.

For me, my practice began to show me personal gifts I never knew I had. I want to make it clear that these gifts are not necessarily part of Reiki. After attunements I received during my training, I was shocked to discover that I had psychic abilities that began to reveal themselves. I also started to see into the past lives of my clients when information was needed in the present that was contained in their past. Then, as time went on, I also began to realize I could communicate with the deceased relatives of my clients.

Because Reiki provides access to so much that is spiritual in nature, you can see why it would be a doorway to those who have died. But it isn't a doorway that opens for all Reiki practitioners—we all have our unique gifts. I wish to point out here that if any gifts present themselves to you that you don't feel a connection to at present, there is no need to incorporate them into your life or use them in your Reiki practice, should you become a practitioner. For example, I have taught Reiki to doctors who are pure scientists with no desire to work with anything even slightly metaphysical in nature, so something like conversing with the deceased would not be of interest to them!

When dealing with Reiki, everything is always entirely up to you. What you will use now, put off until later, or never take advantage of is your business and yours alone.

No one will ever judge your personal choices, and with no judgment ever being made about what you choose, you can freely move forward in whatever way feels comfortable to you.

I know there are many people out there who doubt that we live in a world with unseen forces all around us. But on a daily basis we interact with things we can't see: radio waves, ultraviolet rays, sound waves, and even microscopic bacteria. Modern science has helped us to identify that these things are real. After twenty years in my line of work, I'm here to tell you that we're surrounded by spirits as well. When I do a session, I'm essentially opening myself up to all the "good guys" of the spirit world. These are energy beings, like angels, who are the living consciousness of love. This, by the way, is why a Reiki master is never drained. We are not "giving" anything from within ourselves; we are channeling universal energy. As I feel the energy streaming through me, I often see white light flickering behind my closed eyes, especially when the client is taking in massive amounts of energy. On the other hand, if a client is "blocked," I can't feel or see much of anything at all. When this happens, I stay very still and wait with my hands over that particular spot on their bodies until the blockage hopefully dissolves.

Now that I've been working so long with Reiki, often when I'm treating people, I can know more about them than perhaps they understand about themselves. As the energy comes through and I open myself to it and to them, I can often hear spirit whispering the dreams they've buried deep in their hearts, and I become aware of the true and unique capacity they possess to do something, offer something, or create something for the world. "You might consider signing up for a writing class," I might tell them, or "Have you ever thought about taking a trip to Spain?" And most of the time, if they listen, if they do it, it ends up changing their lives.

Although not technically part of Reiki, these are my own personal gifts that came awake with my Reiki attunements and now bring deep meaning to my life. I decided to accept them and to use them whenever appropriate to assist the people who come to me. These are wonderful gifts to have, but let me be clear: they are not part of Reiki itself, nor are they necessary components for the receiving or giving of this loving energy.

Every kind of person from every walk of life is welcomed into the love that is Reiki. My clients have been sick, well, stressed, heartbroken, spiritual, nonspiritual, religious, dying, in hospitals, in other countries, and everything in between. My students have likewise been from every background and live throughout the world.

Reiki will strengthen any current practice you might have and can be used in combination with other things. For example, some of those who have studied Reiki with me are Yoga teachers who share it while physically touching the bodies of their students as they correct their Yoga postures. Reiki can likewise be used in conjunction with all types of massage. Nurses study Reiki and use it to soothe the patients in their care.

Here's another bit of wonderful news: With Reiki, you cannot make a mistake! You just have to show up. Reiki does the rest.

We all have the right to connect with our spirit guides. What follows is a meditation that will connect you to your very own Reiki master in spirit. Making this connection will be valuable to you as you go along. Please understand that it's not necessary to know your Reiki master in spirit in order to receive a Reiki session. Still, every person interested in Reiki can make a personal connection with a guide. This is a spirit who is the overseer of your Reiki experiences and is invaluable to those of us who practice Reiki. This guide can show itself to you in any form imaginable: It can be a person who once lived that you knew or never knew. It can be an angel, a light, or something else entirely. Regardless of how it shows itself, your Reiki master in spirit is a powerful being on whom you can depend. You may wish to record the following meditation, or have someone read it to you.

Guided Meditation: Meeting Your Reiki Master in Spirit

Part One: Breathing Practice

This meditation can be done either sitting or lying down. Get comfortable, with your spine straight. Close your eyes; notice, as you breathe in and out, how the air passes through your nose and watch as the air goes into your lungs. If your mind sends up thoughts, think to yourself, *I wonder what my next thought will be.* This will usually still the mind, but if you are still thinking, try to simply watch your thoughts as if they are clouds passing across the sky. Begin breathing in to the count of four, hold for four counts, and exhale for eight counts. Count as fast or as slow as is comfortable for you.

Do this four-four-eight breathing pattern for ten rounds, marking the completion of each round by counting on your fingers as you complete each exhalation. Once you count out ten rounds, let your breathing return back to normal.

Part Two: Accessing Golden Light

Now imagine a beautiful, golden, sparkling light beginning to form around your head and upper body. It can look as bright as early morning or as buttery and warming as late afternoon sunshine. Allow this glittering golden light to grow in size to surround you. The sparkles held within this light are the energies of everything positive: love, compassion, forgiveness, kindness, wholeness, tenderness, and every other wonderful thing you can think of.

Let the golden light continue to expand and extend outward, growing in size, flooding that space around you, your aura, with beautiful light. No physical object can interfere with this expansion—not walls, floors, objects, or other people. Your aura, six feet in all directions around you, is your very own unique and specific vibration. Allow that space to fill up with the light.

Now, as you breathe in, the golden light around you is traveling on the oxygen and enters your body. The light-filled oxygen fills your lungs as you breathe. The energy of golden light travels through your bloodstream, bringing blessings to every nook and cranny of your body—soothing you, nurturing you, and raising your vibration with every breath that you take.

Notice how you feel inside as you continue to breathe in the golden light. You are whole. You are nurtured from the inside out. The golden light is the energy of living consciousness, energy full of blessings, just for you. Allow yourself to be at peace. Envision yourself glowing and vibrant. Feel inside yourself as you breathe. Know that in this very moment, you are doing everything you can to bring glorious perfection into your life. Experience yourself as happy and peaceful.

Part Three: Meeting your Reiki Master in Spirit

Float for a moment in peace. Now watch your body breathing. You breathe twenty-four hours a day, three hundred and sixty-five days a year without noticing. Take this moment to watch. Be an observer as your body breathes. Now, using your ability to pretend, make believe that the observer is floating out the top of your head until you see, hear, sense, feel or just know yourself to be standing outside a "hobbit-like" door that is built in the side of a hill. Notice what the door looks like and what it seems to be made of. Knock on the door nine times, and state your name; then say, *I've come to meet my Reiki master in spirit, please.* The door creaks open and you step inside. You are welcomed into this place by its guardian. Is the guardian a person, or a light, or an animal? Can you see, hear, sense, feel, or just know what or who the guardian is? You notice that you are inside an enormous cave, with doors on every wall, even on the ceiling. All the doors lead to different guides. One of these doors leads to your Reiki master in spirit. Without thinking about it, just walk over to one of the doors.

Aha! Your higher Self knew exactly what to do, because this is, in fact, the one that leads right to where you want to go. What does the door look like? What is it made of? Take notice. Go ahead and open the door. Step through and notice what kind of hallway you are now in. Is the background filled with light, or is it mysterious? Are there trees or any other things from nature here in the corridor? Walk slowly and notice everything around you. Pause. Notice how you feel. Can you sense warmth? Do you hear anything? Go all the way down the corridor until you come to a mist, and then you stop. Notice how the mist is thick, like fog. This is the mystical doorway to the realm where your Reiki master in spirit is waiting for you. There is no telling how long this guide has been waiting to meet you, but the love this guide has for you is how it would be if you were a long-lost child, missing for years and not expected to be seen again, who has finally come home. That's the kind of energy and love that this guide has for you.

Before you go through the misty doorway, mentally project, *I ask my Reiki master in spirit to appear before me, in a way I can easily understand and identify with. Please show yourself to me in a way I can embrace with my whole heart.*

Now walk through the mist. You enter into a place of brilliant light; notice where you are. In the center of this place is your Reiki master in spirit. You walk up to this being and greet it in whatever way seems right. It invites you to sit before it, and it sits in front of you. You can witness how happy it is (perhaps tears in its eyes, or a vibration that is full of love and joy, for example). Your Reiki master in spirit reaches over to take your hands. You feel the beautiful energy of love flowing through its hands into you, and that power spreads throughout your body. Your heart is filled with happiness to be in the presence of one who so obviously cares for you.

Sit with your Reiki master in spirit for as long as you like.

Now it is time to go back to your current life as a human on earth. You can come back to be with your Reiki master in spirit whenever you want to. Because this is one of your spirit guides, whenever you think of your Reiki master in spirit, it will be with you instantly. So just for now, say good-bye in whatever way feels appropriate: bow, hug, shake hands, while from the center of your heart, you say, *Thank you* to your Reiki master in spirit for welcoming you, and for all it will be doing for you in the future.

Turn around and go back through the mist into the passageway that is mysterious or filled with light. Travel all the way back to the door and come back into the cave. Thank the guardian for receiving you. As you reopen the hobbit-like door, take a deep breath and as you exhale, come back into your body just where you are in time and space. Feel yourself back inside your body. Feel your body breathing. Notice your belly and chest rising.

Welcome back! Having connected with your Reiki master in spirit will change you in profound ways. Trust your Self. Your Self is now activated by the power of what might be the most constant guide and guardian of your life. This has been true for me. I pray that it will be the same gift for you as you develop a relationship with your Reiki master in spirit by simply thinking of this being on a daily basis. Repeat this meditation whenever you like, as much as you want to.

Surgeons must be very careful when they take the knife!
Underneath their fine incisions Stirs the Culprit—Life!

—*Emily Dickinson,*
108, Complete Poems of Emily Dickinson[8]

CHAPTER 2

Matters of the Heart

Dr. Oz burst through the swinging doors.

"Good morning everyone!" His voice echoed in the flourescent light-filled operating room as it came alive, buzzing with anticipation. Scrubbed and gloved, he gave me a reassuring nod as he swept by, moving toward the head of the operating table.

"Is everybody ready? Because in the next two minutes, I'm gonna open up her chest."

Oh dear God. Did he have to say it like that?

I felt the telltale signs of a faint creeping in: blood and guts have never been my specialty and I already had flutters in my stomach just from being inside a hospital. I'd been sitting on a stool at my client's feet, with chills of icy air running up my arms. Now, taking a deep breath, I maneuvered my way to Susanna's head, stepping carefully over the tubes and wires that connected her to her life support system for the next five hours.

Here in the New York-Presbyterian Hospital/Columbia University Medical Center, as she lay shrouded under drapes of blue material, it was difficult to recognize the woman I'd come to know and love as a client. An overlay of plastic sealed off everything including her face, the shiny blue cocoon secured with clamps to the tubes that rose up around the table and over her head.

As Dr. Oz readied himself to mend Susanna's heart, I placed my hands gently across the crown of her head, closed my eyes, and began the age-old practice that has become like second nature to me.

For the past twenty years, I've been listening to people's bodies. When I work on a person, I listen with my ears, my senses, and my hands. In truth, my hands tell me things the clients don't even know about themselves. My clients' bodies talk, and in learning to listen, I've come to understand a great deal about the human body and how it functions. You see, we rely on our bodies to absorb an awful lot of wear and tear: walking, running, dancing, eating, thinking (lest we forget, our brains are part of our bodies), processing, even aging. It handles colds, flus, and other illnesses that attack on a daily basis. We all know that when our bodies can no longer ward off the barrage of free radicals, pollution, bad vibes from others, toxins, worry, stress, etc., we get sick. But in listening to our bodies through the practice of Reiki, I've learned that the body doesn't just get ill due to an airborne virus or the daily demands we place on it. In some cases, the body gets sick as a last resort to gain attention, because the life itself is crying out for help.

Disease. It's a word we're so familiar with, but we seldom stop to think about its origin. Broken apart, it is *dis-ease*—a sense of being uncomfortable, unwell, hurt, sick, or vulnerable. When our natural state of balance is thrown off, we get sick. But what many people don't recognize is that our physical bodies are not solely affected by physical things like germs. Scientific studies have proven time and time again that emotions like stress, anger, and depression affect our bodies, too. The Mayo Clinic staff has authored articles like the one entitled "Forgiveness: Letting Go of Grudges and Bitterness,"[9] for example, and another, "Meditation: A Simple, Fast Way to Reduce Stress,"[10] in an effort to raise awareness about the effects of negative emotions on our health and how to remedy them.

Stress, of which so many seem to be under the influence, can cause headaches, chest pain, back pain, decreased immune response, high blood pressure, and even heart disease. When we're aware of the consequences of not properly handling our emotions, we can see there are many things that come up in life that can throw off our natural equilibrium. Recent studies have shown that women in unhappy marriages are much more likely to develop high blood pressure, high cholesterol, and heart disease. Things like heartbreak, divorce, abuse, or simple loneliness *do* affect your health. And when we look at it this way, we can understand that much sickness and disease might actually be preventable. Dis-ease is really just an opening through which illness slips into the body. Without dis-ease, there is far less opportunity for disease. And that is a reality, my friends.

Perfect health requires a symphony of physical, emotional, mental, and spiritual well-being. It can be achieved, but to achieve it we have to start looking beyond just our physical selves. We have a tool that treats not just the physical manifestations of disease, but also the causes of disease. Reiki has the ability to treat disease at its very root: it treats both the injury or sickness and the spirit.

I don't believe Reiki is going to solve all of our health-care problems; doctors are everyday miracle workers putting us back together, finding cures, and saving lives. Reiki can't stop a much-needed amputation from becoming a necessity, but it can address the devastating sense of loss and help remaining tissues heal much more quickly. As a Reiki master, I bring this other dimension of health to the table: many sicknesses and injuries originate in realms that most doctors and scientists don't inhabit, and will quite possibly never be able to measure.

Susanna and I felt connected to each other from the moment we were introduced. She was brought to one of my meditation classes by a friend, and I liked Susanna immediately. She had a nurturing energy to her that felt contagious, her bright blue eyes and beautiful smile radiating warmth and calm direction. I wasn't surprised when she told me that she'd been working as a life coach for the past several years; she seemed the perfect mix of brilliant, inspirational, and kind to help guide people to their ultimate potential. She decided to try Reiki due to a car accident that caused a neck injury from which she had never fully recovered. Besides our sessions, we'd often get together for lunch on the Upper West Side, and as we got to know each other I learned that Susanna had lost her sister to cancer, leaving behind two young girls whom Susanna loved like daughters. We'd even started using the same hairdresser. Susanna, *tsk*ing over my unruly curls, insisted I meet her stylist who specialized in curly hair.

But now I was with her in the operating room, her life on the line, my sole responsibility being to maintain the flow of Reiki energy into her for the next several hours while Dr. Oz and his team performed open-heart surgery. My hands placed gently on Susanna's head, I looked at him now. Flanked by his OR team, his gaze was radiating intensity and focus, and his determination gave me confidence. I'd never had a client of mine ask that I step into an operating room before, and Dr. Mehmet Oz was the first surgeon in the world of Western medicine ever to allow a person like me into his operating theater to perform Reiki during surgery.

"Here we go," he said softly. Letting out a deep breath I hadn't known I'd been holding, I once again closed my eyes and let the Reiki flow. Even as I opened up to the gentle warm waves of light that began passing through me, I could feel Susanna's energy beneath my hands: her clear-headed and uncomplicated affection for others, the depth of her connection to her husband and the two charming nieces she loved as her own, and the get-up-and-go energy she shared with the people who invited her to help them transform.

I was here, in this operating room, helping Susanna because I cared for her. But it wasn't easy. I'd almost said I couldn't do it. For me, hospitals still brought feelings of terror that were instilled in me during my surprise tonsillectomy all those long years ago. Operating rooms were cold, exacting rooms where tender skin yielded to cutting steel, and now I found myself deep in the bowels of the last place I wanted to be, helping another woman fight for her life.

Susanna and I had been friends for over a year before we discovered she needed open-heart surgery. After our first session together, she decided to use Reiki just to support her general well-being, and thought of treatments primarily as a relaxation tool, as there are elements of Reiki akin to meditation. It's really the first level of benefit that Reiki offers. It became clear to me in our first few sessions that there was some type of issue in her chest. When I moved my hands over it, I could feel a perplexing pressure and tightness around the area of her heart.

Often when I encounter a blockage like Susanna's—a place where the energy instead of flowing seems to just stick—I'll silently ask my spirit guides to tell me what's wrong. I'll "hear" an answer in my mind. In this case, when I closed my eyes and placed my hands on a place of concern and I asked, *What exactly is going on here?* an image flashed in my mind of Susanna's heart with a thorn stuck in its side. Interesting. It wasn't a literal thorn, of course; it was a symbolic one. As I wondered what this could mean, how this had come to be, how her heart had been damaged, a scene unfolded before me.

I saw a woman who resembled Susanna sitting in a chair, gazing out through a thick and very old-looking windowpane. I recognized her though she was wearing old-fashioned clothing, and her face looked slightly different than the woman I knew now—a longer nose and darker hair. I was seeing Susanna in another lifetime. Her face was soaked with tears. Suddenly I felt a tidal wave of sorrow, a physical sensation so deep I wanted to clutch my own chest for fear my heart was splitting in two. In that moment, I could feel that she was grieving the loss of a man she loved almost more than life itself. I couldn't tell whether he'd died, been taken away, or left, but the pain of it was enough to take my breath away. In my line of work, we believe that some emotional injuries or pain can cause spiritual wounds that can affect us so deeply we actually carry them with us into future lifetimes. This hurt stays with us until we can finally find a way to heal it, learn to grow, and move on.

Now I couldn't help but wonder: had Susanna carried this devastating loss with her into her current life? When the session ended, I told Susanna what I experienced, but she didn't know quite what to make of it. I thought for a moment. "What about in this lifetime?" I asked. "Could anything have caused you this amount of hurt?"

I waited as she considered this. Still sleepy from the session, it took a moment before her blue eyes grew sorrowful. "Well, I know I haven't mentioned this, but my dad died when my sister and I were little. It was completely unexpected."

"Oh, Susanna, I'm so sorry. I had no idea…"

"No, no. I didn't want to talk about it. As it is, we talk about my sister having passed away so much . . ." She blew her nose into the tissue I offered.

"Well, that's ridiculous. We're friends. I want to know these things about you. I'm so sorry you lost your father as just a little girl."

Now it began to make sense to me. This poor woman's heart had taken an emotional toll from the abandonment of deeply cherished men in two lifetimes, not to mention the devastating loss of her only sister. She needed to find a way to heal these past hurts, or I worried that they were going to make her physically ill. I knew that Reiki could help her heal, but I couldn't shake the image of the thorn in her heart from my mind. Had the damage already been done?

A few months later, she told me she'd seen some specialists, and they all agreed that something was wrong with her heart. Worst of all, they were going to have to open her up to find out what it was, and she had to pick which surgeon she felt she could trust with her life. She was on edge when she came for her next session, her brow furrowed, and I could tell she wanted to discuss not just her Reiki options as she moved forward into this new territory, but what surgeon she should use. Although I would never advise a client regarding such an important decision, it helped her to discuss it with me, because my neutrality gave her the space in which she could hear herself speak what was in her heart.

"There's one doctor who really stood out to me," she confided as she leaned back in my office chair.

"Okay, why? What did you like about him?"

She screwed her face up a moment. "Well, I guess I sensed that he really believes in the whole mind–body connection."

"Seriously? Susanna, that's amazing. And pretty rare."

"I know … it is rare. But the thing is, I have to go in to surgery next week."

Now I began to feel a wave of panic rising from her. "Perhaps that's not a bad thing," I reassured her. "Who is it?"

"Dr. Mehmet Oz," she offered.

I blinked, surprised. I couldn't help but take heart in her good fortune. This was a doctor whose name was known to our city. I had read a *New York Times* article by Chip Brown entitled "The Experiments of Dr. Oz" explaining his use of alternative therapies to help his patients.[11] All of New York had held its collective breath while Dr. Oz had performed heart replacement surgery on Frank Torre during the Yankee World Series victory in 1996. He was a surgeon of incredible renown with a legendary body of work. I'd devoured his book, *Healing from the Heart: How Unconventional Wisdom Unleashes the Power of Modern Medicine*, which detailed his motivation behind offering alternative health practices to his patients. For that fact alone, without having ever met him, I was a tremendous fan.

"So, if Dr. Oz is such a supporter of alternative medicine," she began, "do you think he'd allow you to be with me in the operating room?"

No, I thought. And that's exactly what I said. I wanted so badly to be there for Susanna, but I didn't know Dr. Oz personally, and I had no idea if he even knew about Reiki, or what having a Reiki master present might contribute to open-heart surgery. Not to mention my squeamishness; I have to battle my gag reflex to deal with the tiniest wound on my finger. Bearing witness to a chest cavity being pried open was definitely beyond the realm of my capabilities. But Susanna seemed so terrified. If she truly wanted me there, how could I deny her? During the Reiki session, I had the overwhelming feeling that I needed to be brave. At the end of the session, I said to Susanna, "Tell you what. Why don't you bring my résumé with you to your next appointment, and we can see what he says."

That afternoon was a typical day. A new client was coming in for treatment post shoulder surgery, followed by a regular client who was an actor suffering from depression after ending a seven-year relationship. Wanting to be fully present for them, I kept my absent-minded wondering about Susanna's request for Dr. Oz between sessions only. It seemed impossible, but what would I do if he actually said yes? I had an obligation to help my client and a strong desire to help my friend, but underneath it all I was afraid I wasn't up to it. I'd never faced losing a client—or a friend—before my very eyes. Part of me knew that if that was her destiny, I'd end up having to say goodbye right there in the OR. But finally, it was that very thought that made the decision easy. I knew Susanna was more terrified than I could ever be. I wanted to do whatever I could.

When Dr. Oz gave the okay, I was stunned and excited, but mostly anxious. What would the doctors think of me? What if I fainted? And what on earth does someone wear into the operating room with Dr. Mehmet Oz? But weighing most heavily on my mind was Susanna. All I wanted was for her to make it through this procedure with flying colors. So few Reiki masters work in life or death situations, I had no idea what to expect or how to behave.

But there I was. As Susanna was lifted onto the operating table, I felt her anxiety lodge within me, somewhere near the pit of my stomach. Her hand clasped mine as the anesthesiologists administered their cocktails to bring her slowly under. While becoming more relaxed and eventually sleepy, Susanna spoke softly to me, "Raven, I want to live. There are so many things that I still want to do. Please," she whispered, her eyes heavy. "Keep a space open in this room that contains my future. Please… hold on to my life…"

"I will. I promise I will," I whispered, giving her hand a reassuring squeeze. In the next second, her eyes dropped closed and she was under, so anesthetized that she seemed barely alive. The head OR nurse asked me to sit on a stool at Susanna's feet while they got her ready for the surgery. When the anesthesiologist and a team of technicians began sticking tubes into her just about everywhere, I turned my head, closed my eyes, and began to pray, asking that the OR be sealed in a circle of light and love.

As the operation got under way and the Reiki poured through my hands into the top of Susanna's head, Archangel Gabriel, my Reiki master in spirit, asked me to notice the angels at the ceiling of the room. Gabriel was whispering to me that angels are always in operating rooms. They minister to those who are meant to leave their bodies during surgical procedures and they likewise help to keep others "in" who might want to leave their earthly existence ahead of schedule. Now I could sense there were angels close to the ceiling of the operating room, emitting waves of calm. I was aware of the soft radiance that was their energy of serenity flowing through the top of my head and passing into Susanna through my hands, through the Reiki.

I felt utterly peaceful, and then I heard the electric saw start up. My eyes shot open. This was the moment I had been dreading most of all. All I could imagine was that on the other side of the blue swath of material, a saw was edging closer to her skin. A wave of nausea washed through me and I knew I had to get myself under control. I took a very deep breath and emptied my mind of everything but the intention to be empty so I could fill myself with the highest level of Reiki. With that, I entered its thrall. The conversation of the doctors became background sound as I sank deeper into experiencing the gentle pulsing under my hands as Reiki flowed into Susanna.

An immeasurable amount of time had passed when I became aware of Susanna's life-monitoring sounds; they were growing weak. Startled, I opened my eyes and noticed with panic that every single person in the operating room was standing stock still, all staring at the screens overhead. The lines were straightening out! Although Susanna felt energetically sound, I'd never been in an operating room before. Could she be dying? Dr. Oz must have registered the look of panic on my face out of the corner of his eye, because he turned to me calmly and said, "Raven, we're stopping her heart. We're stopping it on purpose. It has to stop so I can replace the valve."

"Oh, thank you for telling me, Dr. Oz." With relief, I closed my eyes and slipped back into peace. I could hear Dr. Oz pointing out to his staff that Susann's damaged heart valve was a textbook case of severe damage caused by childhood rheumatic fever. It could not be saved. Their conversation about the procedures continued while they worked, until Dr. Oz attained his goal—Susanna's heart was outside her body, lying on her chest as it awaited repair.

"Raven," he offered quietly, "would you like to see Susanna's heart?"

"No thank you, Dr. Oz," I said too quickly. "I know it's there." The look on my face was enough to throw the rest of the occupants in the operating room into an unexpected (but from my point of view, much-needed) burst of laughter.

Susanna's life force stayed strong while the work on her heart continued. It had been more than five hours since she had first closed her eyes, and I looked up to see two tiny paddles being held up, before being placed directly onto her heart.

"Clear." A jolt. I held my breath. My eyes stayed fixed on Dr. Oz, whose face lit up with a joyous smile. He turned toward me and said, "Raven! We've already got a heartbeat!"

Every tense muscle in me gave way in relief as I tilted my gaze toward the ceiling. *Thank you*, I thought, expressing my gratitude to the angels and the spirits who had helped us that day.

Some might say—and of course they'd be right—that Susanna needed a heart valve replaced due to a childhood bout of rheumatic fever. But by the time I stood in that OR, I'd seen enough illness to register the connection. Had the rheumatic fever Susanna suffered as a child been merely a physical symptom of a deeper emotional pain, or dis-ease? Perhaps this surgery had given her a chance to reevaluate her life in a way that could finally allow those old wounds to heal. She was forced to take stock of what was truly important to her, just how many people truly loved her, and how she wanted to spend whatever time she'd been allotted here on earth.

Looking down at the blue-shrouded form below me, I realized Susanna was indeed bound in a cocoon, in every sense of the word. What decisions might she make differently once she emerged from her sleep? How might Susanna, through a redefined commitment to living her best life, reach out and inspire others who themselves were destined to change?

As I stood with Susanna, witnessing another woman in her own private fight for her life, I was struck by how astonishing life truly is. Even in our darkest moments, if we can claw ourselves toward home, toward taking care of ourselves, something, some beautiful force, will truly sweep in to ensure we end up right where we need to be. I am not that force, merely an instrument of it—a powerful role nonetheless. History is full of examples of leaders and heroes that were called to be living instruments of God's, or the universe's, love: Joan of Arc, Jesus, the Dali Lama, Dr. Martin Luther King Jr., Mother Teresa, etc. It's an ancient idea, far older than any religion that currently exists, though even the Prayer of St. Francis, in the Catholic tradition, does ask God to "make me an instrument of your peace." In other words, a vessel. We are here to help each other.

In my opinion, every single one of us walking the soil of planet Earth right now has a purpose. Some of us have no idea what our purpose in life is. Others make themselves crazy trying to figure out what their purpose could possibly be. And still others seem to be roaming the world without knowing or caring that they have a purpose, a reason to be alive. Susanna's being a life coach and having to undergo a potentially life-ending surgery was no accident. It was another step on her life's journey toward finding and fulfilling her purpose: helping to inspire others to make life-altering changes. We each have a unique path to finding our purpose in life. For those with an intensely spiritual purpose, that path could lead them to becoming a prophet, shaman, guru, yogi, or priest—all different methods of developing a deep connection with the spiritual world.

My path led me to Reiki. I'm incredibly blessed to have reached the point where I can be a conduit for love, even under circumstances that are sometimes uncomfortable or even scary. Reiki gives me the strength to tap into my own courage. On that day when I woke up in the hospital crib after the horrors of my surprise tonsillectomy, I never could have imagined that someday I'd be helping others learn to heal, even standing in one of the scariest places in the world to me, next to one of the most famous surgeons of our time, helping another woman find her way home.

After Susanna's surgery, much to my complete surprise, Dr. Oz invited me to join his research team. I was stunned, but as I was to discover, he was leading the Columbia Complementary Medicine Program. The research being done by the team was helping to further patients being able to receive an ever-widening array of alternative therapies along with regular allopathic care. Dr. Oz had a serious interest in all things alternative, and was very intrigued by Reiki, which he quickly dubbed "energy medicine." But I still didn't know why I was now part of the research team. It took a bit of time before this mystery even came close to being solved for me.

On Tuesdays I would take the Number One subway train from West 72nd Street to the 168th Street stop during the early-morning rush hour. Squished in like sardines, I was usually standing (sitting was not an option) next to other people who were also headed up to the hospital. The doors would open at 168th Street and we would spill out onto the platform, cross the walking bridge over the tracks, and take the massive commuter elevator up to street level. I'd make my way down the gauntlet of breakfast vendors along 168th Street, grabbing a cup of coffee on my way. Then I'd cross Fort Washington Street, go through the revolving doors of the glass-fronted lobby of the Milstein Hospital Building, and to security I would say, "I'm going to

Dr. Oz's office." Up in the elevator I would go, with my entry pass into the land of Oz.

I pinched myself every single week, because I just couldn't believe my sheer luck, or whatever it was that had arranged for me to be there. From 8:30 to 9:00 a.m. those mornings, I would sit around the shiny dark wooden conference table in Dr. Oz's modest but comfortable conference room, surrounded by some of the most celebrated doctors and research scientists in the world. Dr. Oz would chair the meetings, often dressed in scrubs because Tuesdays were busy days for him in the OR. I listened to the updates on all the experiments being conducted and cheered along with everyone else when it was announced that certain studies had been accepted for publication in medical journals. Research doctors were investigating everything from the effects of prayer to the benefits of music, chelation therapy, aromatherapy, magnets, and everything in between. All of these efforts resulted in science backing up the alternative treatments that were being made available to patients.

I was put on a list of hospital-approved practitioners, and that fact led me to work on a medical drama beyond the scope of what I even thought was possible. I found it amazing to be called in on a case related to a heart matter, though not the heart directly.

Pulmonary circulation is the movement of blood from the heart, to the lungs, and back to the heart again in the overall circulatory system. The heart and lungs work together to cleanse the blood and supply it with the oxygen necessary to keep a body alive. Sean was a client who had heard of me through Dr. Oz's program; he was facing a double lung transplant and wished for extra help going through the process. He called me about Reiki. As we spoke about what I do, his voice was very low and raspy, which led me to believe he was a smoker, and based on that, I imagined he must be an older gentleman. Who else would need not just one, but two lungs? I had never heard of such a medical marvel and was amazed that such a procedure existed. We decided it would be best for us to meet in person to discuss his situation, the Reiki options, and what I could ultimately provide. He invited me to come to his home because he was quite ill and was not able to travel easily, assuring me that his girlfriend would be looking forward to meeting me as well.

I arrived at their beautiful Greenwich Village apartment and was so surprised to be greeted by a very young and handsome man in his twenties with blond hair and blue eyes, though they were dulled by sickness. Standing next to him was his beautiful girlfriend, Gwyneth, with long, flowing black hair and a beautiful smile. Sean explained that he had stage-IV lung cancer. He grew up living in a bedroom in the attic of his family's home that, unbeknownst to anyone, had radon gas leaking out that had caused his cancer. He was not responding to any of the treatment options for lung cancer and his last chance for survival was to get a double lung transplant.

When Sean called me, he was at the top of the hospital's list to get new lungs through their transplant program. Although his transplant surgeon was not open to alternative therapies, Sean wanted to know whether Reiki might help him while he was waiting for lungs to become available. Before proceeding into discussing future plans of how we might work together, he wanted to have an initial Reiki session to experience it, if I wouldn't mind using the massage table he kept in his apartment. Of course I was happy to comply.

Gwyneth and I set up the table in their bedroom before she retreated to the living room, giving Sean and me the peace in which he could experience his first-ever Reiki session. Gwyneth kissed him, saying, "Happy Reiki, my darling!" As she left, she turned off the ringer on the phone so that we would not be interrupted by any outside noises.

As the session got under way, waves of beautiful light were flashing behind my eyes and I felt streams of Reiki healing flowing out from my hands and deep into his cells. It was a very powerful session, during which Sean fell asleep, and he never coughed even once during the hour-long treatment. When I woke him up, he asked me, "How long have I been asleep?"

"An hour," I said.

"Are you serious? I always cough and wake myself up about every fifteen minutes." Apparently, coughing was a never-ending sleep interrupter.

Sean was overjoyed to learn that I could perform distance Reiki during his operation and he decided to go for all the options. We set up a schedule of appointments for him and formulated a plan for what we would do when he got "the call." He took all of my phone numbers and I took his.

We decided that I would come to his home once a week because he was too sick to travel at this point. It was during our second Reiki session together that I felt the presence of the young man who would be giving Sean his lungs. He told me they had known each other in a previous lifetime during WWII and had formed a very strong connection to each other. He told me that in that lifetime, Sean had saved *his* life. He wouldn't show me the details of how, but I knew it was extreme, because they had both been seamen on a navy destroyer, and I felt how much they had loved each other in the past. It was a very emotional session.

At that time, we didn't know that it would be a year before lungs became available. When I came on the afternoon of Sean's third session, he and Gwyneth were both waiting for me at the door, hand in hand. They wanted to talk to me about something important, they said. I can't describe the look of love they shared between them that they trusted me to see. Gwyneth asked me, "Raven, can you see if Sean will die during, or right after, the operation?" Her green eyes were filling up with tears. "If you see him dying, would you please just tell us? Because we really love each other so very much, and if it's not going to work out, we want to know. We just won't go through with it. We'll take the time we have and really enjoy each other as much as we can." They looked at each other, then hugged passionately, eventually turning back to me with eyes shining full of simple trust.

I was shocked by their question—no one had ever asked me such a thing before. "Of course, since you have asked me to find out the answer to this, I will do my best. But I don't feel like Sean will die. However, I will ask the Archangel Gabriel and give you whatever message he sends." I assured them both that I was bound by honor to give them whatever message Gabriel gave me, to the best of my ability to convey it, even if the message was what they feared the most.

When I got back to my apartment, I went into deep meditation. I asked Gabriel the question about Sean's surgery outcome, and what was given in answer was an extensive explanation of life, eternity, evolution, blood memory, and many other wondrous things. I quote here just a small part of what was conveyed to me:

There are deep connections between the participants on both sides of a transplant. The one that gives is serving the receiver as well as the higher calling of God. The God consciousness is calling to a soul to come home. The physical pieces left behind can be used wisely by a person ready to receive healing into their life. What we ask is that one be ready to accept the gift by remaining open to the forward movement of their own life. One... can accomplish more of their purpose when one allows themselves to receive what is being offered. Please do your best to help those in your care to receive their healing. One can never heal without acceptance of the gifts given by spirit to all who call to us for healing... All life is connected... Look after those in your care. We will help you with Sean. He will survive—he has work to do! Amen, child. Help him to receive his organs with ease. It may be a hard procedure, but he will win the big fight to survive with joy. Amen.

I typed up this message and mailed it off to them. In my letter that accompanied Gabriel's message, I explained that by this time in my life, the information shared with me by spirit had always proven to be very accurate, and I had every reason to believe Sean should follow Gabriel's instructions to become the best receiver he could possibly be. Sean and Gwyneth shared all this with their closest friends and family members as encouragement to alleviate the apprehension they were all feeling about the operation.

Sean called me the very next Sunday with news that the hospital had notified him that it was time to come in. He was really frightened as he bustled about, organizing the last minute things he needed to take with him to the hospital. I told him not to worry and that I was going to start distance Reiki as soon as possible.

I prepared everything for the distance session, calling Gabriel and all my spirit helpers to me. It wasn't until I felt surrounded and filled to the brim with love that I began the remote healing. I was surprised, because I felt strangely lightheaded and exhausted while sending Reiki, which never happens to me. When I asked Gabriel, *Why am I feeling so strange?* The answer I got was, *It's because your higher Self knows it's not the right time yet.*

A little while later, Sean called. He was overwrought. The lungs of the accident victim had turned out to be too damaged for transplant. He had been waiting on the operating table when his doctor came in to break the news to him.

In order to be the light of hope for Sean that I wished to be, I decided that I needed to go into a deep shamanic journey on Sean's behalf to ask what the spirits had to give as encouragement to me. I wrote everything down I could remember when it was over, and here's what happened.

I started by stating my intention: *I'm seeking healing and wisdom for Sean! I'm seeking healing and wisdom for*

Sean! at least four or five times, then just let go. My inner visions led me onward to where I was standing next to a grizzly bear. The bear was busy catching a fish at the edge of a huge lake. He caught the fish and projected into my mind that he caught it for me. The bear communicated to me that I needed to bite the head off and remember that I was eating its eyes, because the eyes of a salmon are the eyes of wisdom. I bit the head off with a focus on trying to garner the knowledge I needed that was contained in the fish eyes.

I began to cry because I was afraid for Sean. So the bear jumped into the lake and swam with me on its back. We went far out into the water, with me crying all the way. A gateway appeared that looked like the gates to a ranch, only these gates were in the middle of the water and they were made of diamonds. The gates swung open and the bear swam calmly through them.

We arrived on a beach, which was another level of reality. This new place was brilliantly colored, though the colors were all in the darker shades. The colors were surreal—green pine trees were next to trees that were deep blue and purple. The bear conveyed to me that we had arrived safely on the other side of Sean's experience in spite of all my fear and crying. He made me understand that emotions are nothing in the face of true power. I was brought into the spirit dimension of the operating room where Sean's surgery would take place. A wolf was leading a whole pack of wolves and lots of other animals in a wild dance around the operating room. I was told that all the animals dancing were power animals, who were the spiritual helpers not only of Sean, but of the doctors and all other operating room personnel; whether the humans knew about power animals or not, they were still connected to these animals. The animal spirits were creating Sean's safety and healing, and I was told they would keep dancing all the way through the operation.

Then a raven came for me to fly on its back, flanked by two eagles. We flew together into the higher realms. I can't remember much of what was happening there, as the vibration was so fine and otherworldly. But I know I was told that the angels and spirits of the light were also assembling in the operating room to assist and support Sean and the power animals. I saw the OR from a long way off. Archangel Gabriel told me I had to lay myself down before the Light Force Beings who suddenly appeared. I asked Gabriel for healing; I asked him to heal me of my fear and to fill me up with greater light. I felt the light intensify inside me for several minutes.

Next, the bear was leaning over me. He took his claw and cut a huge cross in my chest. There was no physical pain, but I understood that I was going through a surrogate operation in advance for Sean. Once I was cut open, the bear tore out my poisoned lungs with his sharp teeth. Once all the poisoned tissue was out, new lungs that looked like light-filled balloons were put in place. The bear breathed more and more light into my lungs until everyone present was satisfied at their level of illumination. Then I was sewn back together by angelic spirits, and I found myself rising up from the operating table, as Sean. I felt Sean's victory inside me as if it were my own, and I knew beyond doubt that Sean would survive and be overjoyed at breathing normally again.

I asked for Sean to have a secure feeling after the operation because I knew that he was afraid of what would happen after the surgery. The spirits said to relax. They would take care of everything. They advised me to simply think of Sean surrounded by and full of Light. Next I sent out a "thank you" to the person who would be giving their lungs. I prayed for him to have a safe journey home, and for bands of angels to continuously surround him. I made this prayer over and over. Then I saw a smiling face peeking over a piece of fabric. I saw that it was the lung giver, smiling and helping Sean to survive and to heal quickly.

In the next breath, I was back in my living room in New York City. With a heart full of gratitude, I wrote everything down, but not before saying "thank you" to Gabriel and to all the spirits who had blessed me with such visions.

It was wonderful to get the information that seemed to indicate that Sean would survive, but it's important to note that a very different outcome could have been the true healing that was needed. In other words, using advice from the spirits and giving Reiki must never come from the ego's goal to cure, but with the intention to heal no matter what that might look like. It was just as likely that I would have received word on how to ease Sean into death, if that is what he needed to do.

By now, Sean and I had formed a very close bond, so I felt safe telling him about my journey and sharing with him what the spirits had said. The details helped him and Gwyneth to feel much more positive and to keep their hopes up while they waited.

Before we knew it, it was heading toward autumn. Sean called me from the hospital; he had been brought in an ambulance and was too ill to be released. I went to see him that very night. It was a Friday, and I walked into a very tearful scene in the hall outside his room. Gwyneth sobbed uncontrollably in the arms of Sean's mother, who was in no better shape. The doctor had just told the family that Sean was going to die—he wouldn't make it through the night. Their anguish was too much for me, and not knowing what else to say or do, I just went into Sean's room to be with him. His condition was shocking. With eyes closed, his sweat drenched blond hair was spread out across the white pillow and he was in terrible pain. I had such a moment of doubt. How was this ever going to work out? Were the spirits joking? How was this going to come to the promised happy ending, when it was so apparent to everyone that Sean might not live until the morning? I began to administer Reiki to him as he feverishly moaned. At one point he had to sit up. He coughed so hard, and for so long, that I wondered if he would ever stop. In the end, he fell asleep during his session. I greatly doubted myself, and I felt like everything I believed in was on the line. Even after all the Reiki I was able to give, in sleep Sean looked totally exhausted, very, very sick, and so close to death…

Early the next morning my husband and I took our dog, Echo, for a walk in Central Park. We stopped to hear some joyous music being played in the Band Shell. While sitting there on a bench in the warm sunshine, I tearfully prayed, "Please let Sean get his lungs today." While I was making my prayer, Gwyneth was with Sean in his hospital room. His doctor came in, shocked that he had survived the night, and much to Gwyneth's complete surprise, the doctor began to pray to Jesus and Mary, asking that lungs for Sean would come right away.

When Michael and I got home from the park with Echo, there was a red light flashing, letting us know we had a message. It was Gwyneth. When I called her back, she told me that Sean's transplant surgeon was getting on a Lear Jet to see the donated lungs. Sean had asked me to please come to the hospital immediately. She explained that the doctor was so shocked by the fact that Sean had lived through the night after a Reiki session that he changed his mind and said I could go into the operating room after all. Before we hung up,

Gwyneth went on to say that after his Reiki session the night before, Sean had the best night's sleep of the past few months.

Oh dear, I was going back into the operating room again? I knew it was a privilege for me to be allowed in, but to be notified so last minute had not afforded me the opportunity to get myself prepared for it. However, that was just too bad. We were all at the doorway that everyone had been praying for.

When I got to the hospital, Sean's family stood around his bed and Gwyneth was lying in the bed next to him, holding him in her arms. I felt my eyes start to fill up with tears, and forbade myself to cry. There was a surgery coordinator who was organizing all the details for the operation, putting two surgery teams on red alert. She was waiting for final word from Sean's transplant surgeon, who had flown to a hospital somewhere in the South to determine whether or not the lungs were really transplantable.

In transplant surgery, time is of the essence. In this case, a separate surgical team was needed to remove Sean's lungs while the transplant surgeon was in transit. The surgery coordinator assembled the lung-removal team first. She asked the doctor in charge of the removal if I could go into the operating room to give Reiki to Sean. Her request was a total shock to him. Not only had he never heard of Reiki, this was the first news he had that anything out of the ordinary was being allowed. I guess the surgery coordinator must have presented a powerful case, because the doctor finally agreed to let me into the OR, but I could only stay until Sean was under anesthesia. Then the doctor wanted me to leave while he performed his part of the surgery. He told the coordinator, "If the other doctor wants her in there for the transplant, he'll have to confirm that when he gets here with the lungs."

I knew I could never enter an operating theater with Sean's surgery already underway. See his whole chest a gaping hole? Oh, no, never. Not ever.

But Sean was so relieved. The most important thing to Sean was that I be allowed in to provide Reiki until he went to sleep.

News came that the lungs were in great shape and that Sean would be getting the surgery. By now, the outside waiting room was full of extended family and close friends, all of whom Sean and Gwyneth called into his room. Sean was too sick to speak, so Gwyneth spoke for him.

"Well, this is it! We're moving ahead. This is Raven, and she is Sean's personal healer. She can teach all of you how to send light to Sean during his surgery. We ask you to do this for us, would you please?"

There wasn't a dry eye in the room.

"Let's all hold hands and Raven will lead us in a prayer." I felt so honored to be of service at a moment of such heartfelt emotion.

When Sean and I entered the brightly lit OR, he was terrified. The nurses and technicians were already poking him with needles and inserting IVs, racing the clock to begin the first of the dual operations. Sean was going to be put under anesthesia soon. The surgeon who was removing the diseased lungs was already scrubbing up in the prep room on the other side of the swinging doors to our left. I asked Sean to please focus on looking directly into my eyes while I held his hand. I sent Reiki through my hand into his, while reassuring him, "Don't worry, Sean. Remember, you are coming through this with flying colors. Gabriel said so." But before I could tell him anything else, he was already asleep. The surgeon was entering the room scrubbed and gloved, and I knew it was time to go. With a catch in my throat, I left Sean in the care of surgery team number one.

In spite of my deep devotion to Sean, I knew I would never be able to enter the OR when the lungs came, no matter what the second doctor said. I knew I would faint. There would be no way around seeing Sean's chest open if I had to walk through those doors during the procedure. So I focused on teaching everyone to send light. I told them:

> *It doesn't matter if you see, hear, sense, feel, or just know this experience, we are all unique. Just embrace however it happens for you. Go into the space in the center of your chest that is your heart chakra. Don't worry if you don't know what your*

heart chakra is; your higher self already knows all the answers, so just follow along. Imagine that you are calling golden light to fill that space in the center of your chest. Let that space become a ball of light that grows larger and larger inside you with each breath, until it fills your whole body... take your time. Now let the light expand even more in size until it moves beyond your skin and into the area around the outside of your body. Let the light become stronger still, intensifying in brilliance... When you feel ready, float the ball of light away from you and tell it to find Sean. See, hear, sense, feel, or just know the ball of golden light leaving the room and traveling. Envision it finding Sean and surrounding his body. Envision the light entering Sean's body and healing him.

Once I taught everyone how to send light to Sean, we all did so in whatever ways felt comfortable. Some of us held hands while sending it. Some of us prayed. Some of us sent light together in groups, and some of us sent light individually. Everyone was involved.

After a while, Gwyneth asked me to go with her to stand in the hallway outside the operating room. We stood together, holding hands and sending light from a place to the right of the entrance doors. I was filling our ball of light up with Reiki symbols by visualizing them and projecting them into the center of the light ball. Then we sent it on into the OR. As we began to slowly move back toward the waiting room, a nurse came out of the operating room. Gwyneth asked if the lungs had come yet. The nurse said she didn't know for sure, but she thought the transplant team was close to arriving at the hospital. We continued walking toward the overpass that led back to the waiting room. Suddenly we heard running feet coming toward us. It was the transplant surgeon and his team! I held my hands up and sent Reiki into the organ cooler as the doctor ran by. He was calling out to us, "Try not to worry! I'll see you later!"

We stood there and I held Gwyneth in my arms as she wept. It felt like a miracle that we were actually there to witness when the lungs meant to save Sean's life were brought to save it!

I stayed at the hospital until about 3:00 a.m. I went home after I finally heard the news that all had gone well, the operation was a success, and Sean was in the recovery room. I left basking in the full knowledge that Sean would be fine. Gwyneth called me in the morning. She said Sean was asking for me. I raced up to the hospital. Sean was in the intensive-care unit, full of tubes. One went down his throat, so he couldn't really speak. "Sean," said Gwyneth softly, "Raven's here." He opened his eyes. A tear rolled down his cheek. His mouth formed the silent words, "Thank you, Raven."

A year later, I danced at their wedding.

One of the first things a Reiki practitioner learns is to hold the intention to be a pure conduit for healing energy to pass through. Mostly this is about surrendering one's attachment to outcome and turning instead to respecting everyone's right to make their own decisions. Intention is a truly powerful force that connects us to the universe. This is because when we establish an intention to do something, it clears a path for energy to flow freely into the physical world from spirit. Your intention claims what type of energy you want to connect to. You want to ensure the energy you are bringing into the world (through you) is pure, beautiful, and healing. If you bring beautiful energy into you, you'll begin to attract that same energy back to you, and your life will begin to shift for the better. You'll meet positive new people, attract exciting and wonderful new opportunities, and your life will begin to flow in ways you can't imagine; like attracts like!

For Reiki practitioners, it's important to know how to surrender to a pure intention to assist, rather than try to manipulate another person's course in life. Deciding the outcome of a Reiki session comes from the ego. None of us has the right to interfere with the choices someone else makes. Sometimes it's hard to resist the urge to suggest Reiki to those we care about. This is especially hard when you witness someone you love destroying themselves with drugs or alcohol. No matter who you are, what you do, or who's around you, ultimately it's necessary to understand that all of life and consciousness throughout the universe has free will.

The following meditation will help harness your own intention to create positive change in your own life and to likewise respect the free will of those around you.

Guided Meditation: The Intention to Allow Healing

Part One: Breathing Practice

This meditation can be done either sitting or lying down. Get comfortable, with your spine straight. Close your eyes; notice, as you breathe in and out, how the air passes through your nose and watch as the air goes into your lungs. If your mind sends up thoughts, think to yourself, *I wonder what my next thought will be.* This will usually still the mind, but if you are still thinking, try to simply watch your thoughts as if they are clouds passing across the sky. Begin breathing in to the count of four, hold for four counts, and exhale for eight counts. Count as fast or as slow as is comfortable for you.

Do this four-four-eight breathing pattern for ten rounds, marking the completion of each round by counting on your fingers as you complete each exhalation. Once you count out ten rounds, let your breathing return to normal.

Part Two: Visualization

Take a moment to imagine you are on a beautiful, warm, breezy beach. See, hear, sense, feel, or just know that the sun is shining upon you, soothing your body. Fill in your experience with as many details as you can. Smell the air. Feel the breeze flowing across your skin. Hear the sea. Know the warmth of the sun soothing your body. Hear gulls. Relax. Take your time.

Think to yourself:

> *Life is beautiful. I am beautiful. I am truly beautiful. I am a child of the universe. I am an expression of beauty as a living thing. My beauty is unique. There is only one "me" through all of time and space. I am so beautiful in my uniqueness. I am beautiful. I am beautiful just because I exist. I allow healing to come into my life in ever-deepening ways. I do not direct it. I allow it to just "be" whatever it needs to be for me.*

Next, think to yourself:

> *All others are beautiful. They are truly beautiful as unique expressions of life in the universe. I am not responsible for anyone else's happiness. I am not here to save anyone. I give myself, and all others, freedom to heal in whatever ways I and they need to. I do not have the answers for any other being on earth.*

To amplify your process, whenever you look in the mirror, take a moment to look into your own eyes. Think to yourself, *I love you. You are just so beautiful! I am beautiful, beautiful, beautiful in my own unique way, as are all others. There is only one of me through all of time and space, and I am beautiful! I am responsible only for myself.*

You can use your own words, but you get the idea.

We must bring our problems to light
in order to be rid of them.
—*Marianne Williamson,* Healing the Soul of America: Reclaiming Our Voices as Spiritual Citizens [12]

CHAPTER 3

Healing the Emotions: Heartache, Grief, and Stress

After Susanna's surgery, when I was part of Dr. Oz's research team at Columbia Presbyterian Hospital, I'll never forget the day when he said to us at one of our meetings, "I cannot discount the fact that [making quote signs with his fingers] 'Mr. Smith' might have had a heart attack because his wife divorced him, which caused him emotional devastation, leading to his body reacting in such a disastrous way. Maybe that same divorce might lead a woman to heart disease. We don't have the ways in which to measure this yet, but I believe energy medicine may be able to help alleviate the kind of pains medicine has no control over." My work had shown me that painful emotions are often the creation point of illness. I was overjoyed to be hearing confirmation in the conference room of someone with such strong credentials.

Reiki provides balance and instills feelings of stability along the rocky road of emotional upheaval. I've had clients come to me suffering from insomnia, anxiety, heart palpitations, headaches, weight gain, weight loss, addiction—all from heartache. Because Reiki is pure, unconditional love, it soothes and comforts one into feelings of safety. From a place of safety, emotional release can naturally occur.

I've had more than my share of clients who are going through romantic breakups. The stories of clients coming for this type of healing are endless. Like Ally, for example, who found out her "boyfriend" was married. What a nightmare when this kind of situation arises! In her case, Ally ended the affair, but her emotions were all over the map. Although she knew it was for the best, she was hurting; her pain was overwhelming her. Her heart was broken with missing her lover, and she was in agony over what her life would become without him. She was miserable.

Holding these emotions in can only harm a person. As Dr. Oz so aptly expressed, one could even develop heart disease from suppressed emotions. Luckily, during her Reiki session, Ally had a tremendous emotional release. It shook out of her body. "Oh, Robert!" she cried out, "How could you do this to me?" Her arms came up as she held herself, rocking back and forth on the table, "How could you lie so? How could you let me love you so much, when you knew you already had a wife?" Torrents of heart-wrenching tears poured out of her. I kept my hands over her upper chest while she cried, until finally she stopped sobbing. Ally seemed to drift away, sinking deep within herself until finally she settled into an inner place of calm.

It is important to note that there is a place inside every one of us where there is peace. This place can be found and experienced during Reiki sessions. I can't tell you the number of times clients have mentioned how serene they feel after sessions, no matter what their current situation might be. In many cases, the feelings of peace remain long after the session is over; it could be for days or even months, and sometimes the relief is permanent. Ally got back on track, and I think part of it was that she knew that she had no choice but to get over this guy. I ran into her about two weeks later.

"Raven, thanks so much! I was able to let go of Robert during our session, and I'm feeling much more hopeful about my life now. I have the courage to move forward."

Happy endings come so often to my breakup Reiki clients that I'm no longer surprised. Why? Well, by now I've figured out that although Reiki is not a love potion, it does in fact fill people up with so much universal love energy that they become magnets, drawing love to them. Like attracts like, so it wasn't long before Ally met the man of her dreams, got married, and moved to Colorado. Believe me, I wasn't shocked!

As I mentioned before, every Reiki practitioner is unique and has their own gifts; for me, experiencing the presence of angelic beings is standard operating procedure. My connection with angels is a gift that awakened in me during my training, and intensified with each Reiki attunement I received therein. The angels often vibrate beautiful energy into and through me—energy that fills me first, and then comes out of my hands and into my client. Over time, I'd become familiar with how angels felt: bright and calming. So the first time that a deceased person "showed up" in the room while I was treating a patient, I felt the energy shift to something new, and it shocked me.

Calvin was an ophthalmologist who came to me on a recommendation from his son, who was a client of mine. As soon as I began his treatment, he instantly fell into a deep sleep, which is a common occurrence when one receives Reiki. It is so relaxing that sleep is one of its natural by-products. Sleep itself promotes healing in the body, so combined with Reiki, the possibilities to heal are endless. I've also come to understand that if the spirit guides have somehow managed to lead a skeptic to a treatment, often times they'll be snoring by the time I count to ten. I believe one of the reasons they fall asleep is not only for proper healing, but also because the conscious mind of a skeptic can work to reject the experience. As a result, such a client often gets spiritually "knocked out," enabling them to receive the healing on another level. This happens so often, in fact, that I now make sure to tell my clients that just because you fall asleep, that does *not* mean the session has less of an effect. People get so worried that they're missing something when they doze off, when in fact I've found it to be exactly the opposite.

Just as quickly as Calvin had fallen asleep, I experienced a spine-chilling feeling. Have you ever been absorbed with something and felt someone enter the room before physically seeing them? Well, that's what this was like. It was as though a stranger had just strolled into the room with Calvin and me.

I sent out the thought, *Who's there*? And with my eyes closed, the hair on the back of my arms began to rise as I received the mental image of an older man with dark hair streaked with gray, standing at the other end of the table from me. But at the same time, I could feel all the years that went into the bond between him and the man on my table as though they were my own. I could feel the pain of how much they missed each other, and the waves of sadness and loss made my heart feel heavy.

There was no question in my mind: this was Calvin's father.

Why is it that you've come here? I asked him silently. To my surprise, I could hear his response in my head.

I want you to tell my boy how much I love him. I wasn't sure how to respond. My Reiki teacher had never warned us about *this*!

Tell him that I'm so much better off now; tell him the pain is gone, he continued.

Raven, I told myself sternly, *there is absolutely no way you're telling this man you've just been chatting with his dead father. He's a medical professional! He's going to think you are absolutely out of your mind!* I squeezed my eyes more tightly shut, trying to (politely) ignore him.

I'm very sorry, but I can't do it, I told his father in my head.

But the stubborn old man wouldn't take no for an answer. *How would you feel,* he communicated to me, *if your father died and someone had a message from him, but that person failed to give it to you because they were afraid?*

Yes, I got his point—it went straight to my heart. Bowing my head, I promised him I'd do my best.

When Calvin woke up at the end of the treatment, I told him as tactfully as I could what I'd experienced, half expecting him to leap up from the table and shout, "My father's not dead—he lives in a condo in Palm Springs!"

But still deeply under the influence of Reiki, Calvin listened attentively and left in what I perceived to be a pensive mood, leaving me wondering if what I said had affected him at all.

So you can imagine that I was floored when Calvin's son came in the following week and told me his dad had been overjoyed by what had happened in our session. Apparently, Calvin's father—my regular client's grandfather—had been very sick before he passed away, and was terrified to die. To make matters worse, his death had been particularly painful and traumatic. Since he passed away, they'd all been feeling at a loss, buried under tremendous amounts of grief, sadness, and anxiety on his behalf, wondering most of all if there was such a thing as life after death. Our session was the catalyst Calvin needed to begin recovering from the loss of his father and continue to heal with the understanding that his father loved him, and that wherever his father was, everything was okay. When left untreated, grief and anxiety can open the door for a whole host of disease, so while it may seem like an immeasurable triumph, I knew that the session would have incredible benefits on a physical level as well.

Calvin's father was my first brush with a deceased spirit, but as I became more practiced at Reiki, these visitations became more frequent. I've seen lives change right there on my table: eyes light up, old wounds heal, all at the gentle word of someone very loved, who now feels far away. The idea that the afterlife is far away is a misconception. I think the spirits of those we love are closer than we assume, guiding us and loving us from their own plane of existence, touching us in ways that we can't always comprehend. I'm blessed that my role in this process can be so clear-cut, and that I can occasionally facilitate communication if there's a message someone on the other side has for my client, to help my client grow. Even when there isn't a spirit presence during a session, at least not a human one, I suspect that our loved ones are somewhere nearby, contributing to the healing light energy that can fill us up and make us whole.

What follows is an interesting case when I used the remote form of distance Reiki at the request of a friend, who put in an SOS call to me. It was a rainy summer's night in 2004 when she called my home. "Raven, my father needs open-heart surgery!"

"Where is he?" I asked.

"He's in a hospital out on Long Island. My family is desperate. He can't get the surgery because his neck veins and arteries are full of plaque."

"What does his doctor have to say about it?"

"He just keeps saying the plaque has to be cleared before the surgeon can operate. Can you please do a distance healing?"

"Ask your father for permission for me to work on him and call me back."

Her father gave his permission. Because it was a distance session, the man's free spirit was able to communicate with me in ways he might not have been able to if he was in my physical presence, me being a complete stranger to him. Instead, during the healing session, I concentrated on moving the plaque out, and along the way, his spirit impressed into my mind what was at the bottom of his health issues. He said, *My heart is broken because my family members can't get along harmoniously. I love all my daughters, but they don't seem to like each other. They are always fighting, not just with each other, but with my wife, too. I'm so sad about this!*

Do you want me to tell your daughter? I asked.

He replied, *Yes, please let her know that the only thing I really care about is love. I want to feel loved and see love around me, love between those that I love the most—my family!*

Okay, I'll tell her. Please, let's move the plaque out so you can have your operation and live to see everyone getting along, okay? I said to him.

Okay!

My friend cried many tears when I revealed to her what her father had told me ... and her dad lived to become another Reiki miracle. His veins and arteries were miraculously cleared in that one distance session. He went on to have his operation and healed quickly, surrounded by smiling daughters and an attentive wife. His dream came true; everyone was getting along harmoniously, because he was able to finally tell someone what was in his heart.

Raphael arrived in my office very embarrassed about being hung over from his previous night of drinking. In our beginning conversation, he told me that his son had just gotten married and that his daughter had been killed ten years before in a car accident. I knew in my heart that he was self-medicating with alcohol to deal with his depression.

"Try not to worry about anything right now," I told him, "Just lie down here and I'll give you some good energy, okay?"

"Yes, good idea, I could use some good energy," he said.

When Raphael was finally stretched out on the table and I began the flow of Reiki, I felt my face tensing in concentration as I tried to understand who or what had just moved into the room. There was a presence standing next to me that was unlike anything I had ever felt. It was a powerfully enlightened male presence, and I somehow knew that it was someone who had been human in the not-so-distant past.

Who are you? I asked. *Can you tell me your name?*

I felt myself shiver with shock when the presence impressed into my mind that his name was Maharishi. It almost knocked my socks off to encounter, right in my office, such a famous Indian guru who had died two years before!

Please tell Raphael that he must resume his meditation practice right away, said Maharishi. *His heart hurts. He is suffering because the marriage of his son reminds him of everything that will never happen on earth for his daughter. He is living in illusion. Tell him his daughter is safe with me. I am taking care of her.*

The energy that was pouring through me was so strong I was almost passing out from the intensity of it, and all this before even ten minutes had gone by! Meanwhile, Raphael was already fast asleep in response to the deep relaxation Reiki brings. As if that wasn't enough, at the end of the session when I was sending Reiki into the bottoms of Raphael's feet, Maharishi's teacher, Guru Dev, arrived. He stood at Raphael's head while Maharishi floated above Raphael's body, sitting in the lotus position with his eyes closed. Love energy poured out of both of them in waves of light.

After the session was over, it took a while for Raphael to come around, and when he did, I asked him, "Raphael, have you formerly done meditation?"

"Oh, yes, I studied under Maharishi in India. I was even with him when the Beatles were there." I know I gasped. I never quite get used to the amazing things that happen during sessions, and I hope I never do.

"Well, Maharishi came, and he said you must begin your meditation practice again right away. He also told me that your daughter is safe and happy. He is taking care of her." Raphael started to cry. He couldn't speak. I knew it was hard for him to be crying in front of me, someone who was basically a stranger, so I handed him some tissues and left to wait in the bathroom while he got himself together. After waiting for what I thought was enough time, I came back.

"Thank you so much, Raven. I will try to get back to my meditation practice, but can we please meet again next week?" And with that, he left my office. That's when I pulled down the shades and sat in the darkened room in my own personal meditation, asking about time and space, life and death, yin and yang. I also gave profound thanks to the two masters who had graced my office with their wonderful energies of pure, unconditional love.

Just like in my own personal story, encountering Reiki shifted Raphael's life in ways we could have never predicted. Not only did he recommit to his meditation practice, as our Reiki sessions continued, he became more and more interested in practicing Reiki himself. He went on to study Reiki with me. During his training, he experienced a beautiful connection with his deceased daughter, which brought him lasting peace.

Raphael was just one example of someone whose life was in crisis mode due to overwhelming emotional upheaval. He was on the road to alcoholism, but Reiki helped him to transform his pain into something really meaningful to him.

Sometimes a person suffers from emotional trauma that comes from another lifetime. Such was the case of Arenda. A beautiful lady of a very exotic nature, Arenda was unique in every way—from the bone structure of her face, to her hairstyle, to the clothes she wore. Arenda was suffering from deep depression that she just couldn't shake. She arrived at my office, downcast and feeling utterly discouraged.

Sitting opposite each other in the comfortable white chairs that grace my office, she confided, "I've taken every antidepressant known to humankind, all to no avail." Her eyes started filling up with tears. "I've taken

Chinese herbs to the tune of many thousands of dollars. I've had three acupuncture sessions a week for eight months straight. And I still feel horrible! You probably can't help me, but I'm desperate. I just don't know what to do anymore. I don't want to keep suffering like this. I want to really live!"

I told her that I would do all I could for her, and invited her onto my table. She lay down on the table, with her amazing hair tucked under her head, and the session got underway. While my hands were over her heart, I had an unexpected vision of a past life when she had been a priestess in a Temple of Isis. In the vision, I saw that she was alive at the end of an era, a time in which the temples were being overtaken by a new religion and shut down. Her temple had been invaded and Arenda had witnessed terrible things. Someone she loved very much was killed before her eyes. I was thankful that I wasn't shown the details, with my abhorrence of violence.

My Reiki master in spirit, Archangel Gabriel, whispered to me that Arenda was suffering because she carried this tragic memory deep inside the inner recesses of her blood memories. Gabriel went on to say that Arenda was feeling very lethargic about everything she was doing, because nothing seemed important enough to inspire her to happiness. She missed being a priestess, with the responsibilities her role carried along with sharing her gifts with others as she had done in that other lifetime long ago. Nothing could compare to the grace and beauty of that other existence.

After the session, I told Arenda what I had seen. Her head bowed, she peered up at me with her dark eyes, nodding in what I could only imagine was her own understanding and recognition that what I said was true. In the way she looked at me, I felt I was giving her important information that made sense to her.

Because I am an ordained priestess in the Fellowship of Isis—an order founded many years ago by Lady Olivia Robertson at Clonegal Castle in Enniscorthy, Ireland—I could point Arenda in the direction of reclaiming her priestess role. I recommended that she begin to reestablish her deep spiritual connection to the Goddess by starting a daily morning practice of reciting the Prayer of Awakening from the book *The Mysteries of Isis: Her Worship & Magick* by DeTraci Regula. I also sent the Midnight Prayer to Isis, and it was now up to Arenda to pursue her own healing by reconnecting with the ways in which she had found happiness in her former life. In a case like hers, Reiki provided her with answers, but the rest was up to her. In the end, this is how it is for all of us. We can either claim our happiness, which is our birthright, or just keep traveling along the same old road doing the same old things with the same old results. However, that isn't usually the case for those who encounter Reiki!

Cathy had recently lost her mother and was very depressed. Heartache made it impossible for her to sleep and the insomnia was making it next to impossible for her to work. A thoughtful friend gifted Cathy with a few Reiki sessions to help her to move forward.

The anger Cathy was experiencing shocked me as I felt it radiate out of her body. It was just so extreme! In order to be effective, I felt I had to ask her about it.

"Cathy, are you mad about something?"

She burst into tears.

"I'm furious at my sister!" Cathy couldn't speak further; she just lay there weeping. Then finally, "My mom was living with my sister in Quebec. We knew Mom was sick, and I asked my sister if I could come for a visit, but she said no, that it wasn't a good time. She said Mom was doing better, and then Mom died before I got to see her!" Cathy continued to cry. Suddenly her body stiffened as she clenched her fists at her sides, gritting her teeth and spitting out, "I hate my sister! I hope she dies! That bitch! I hate her, I hate her, I hate her." She began to crumble and sob even harder than before. This engulfing anguish mixed with rage was what was keeping her up nights. The physical effects were that her rage was causing her to grind her teeth all the time, resulting in pounding headaches.

Cathy was able to have emotional release on my table, and after a few sessions of pure releasing, she felt very comforted by the Reiki. The physical sensations of peace and relaxation were very profound for her. As she became more relaxed, Cathy also began to feel an unexpected connection to angels. She began to experience them surrounding her and soothing her with love.

Even after that initial session, Cathy slept through the night for the first time in the weeks since her mother's death. During the subsequent sessions, her emotional equilibrium was reestablished and she was able to return to work.

Under unique circumstances, and with careful planning, I am sometimes able to do a session in a client's home. It can be like a field trip for me, and I knew Clarissa had a special apartment designed by a famous architect that I wanted to see. Clarissa was an interior designer with a healthy curiosity about Reiki and wanted to experience what it might do for her.

I arrived at Clarissa's interestingly decorated home just as the skies were darkening with rain clouds. We set ourselves up in front of her huge windows and took it as a good sign when flashes of lightning and crashes of thunder got underway just as we began our session. In the first few moments, as I worked on her head, my mind's eye saw a funeral in progress. I felt it was a mother who was being buried. I saw a casket covered with white roses being put into a hearse and wondered if Clarissa had recently lost her mother.

Next I saw Clarissa dressed in black, mourning over an abortion. The spirit of a baby girl lovingly presented itself and conveyed gratitude to Clarissa for the opportunity she had provided to evolve as a soul. The baby told me that she had known in advance that her time was to be short, which was her own choice. The baby's experience had been magnificent in its brevity. She didn't want Clarissa to suffer any more over having had an abortion. The baby suggested that Clarissa perform a ceremony (of her own choosing) in order to release her attachment to its soul.

Please ask Clarissa to release me fully by forgiving herself. She is beautiful through and through, and there is no guilt she should feel about me. I chose her because I knew I would get to be back home, back in the Light, very quickly, the soul said. While I was hearing the voice of the baby in my head, Gabriel was washing me with extra love so I wouldn't cry.

When I discussed all this with Clarissa at the end of the session, she told me that her friend's mother had died, but she and her friend had been in difficulty at that time, so she hadn't attended the funeral. She felt that my seeing it was a message to her that she make amends with her friend and lend him her support. Also, she had in fact had an abortion over which she was suffering. It was comforting to know the details concerning the baby's knowledge in advance that she wouldn't be born into this world at that time.

I saw Clarissa at a class a few weeks later, and she told me that she had followed through on everything from her session. She had dinner with her friend, who was so grateful to have her love during such a trying time. She had also conducted a beautiful ceremony to say goodbye to the baby. Soon after this, Clarissa met a man, got married and had a baby girl, full of vigor, health, and joy!

Emotional distress can have physical ramifications that I witness in a large body of work I do with women who are struggling to conceive. Oh, yes indeed! This is New York City, where women have big careers that match their type-A personalities and drive. It is very common for these ladies to realize that by the time they decide to have children, the clock has ticked for a lot of years. This can cause emotional panic. And although fertility doctors can perform amazing things to promote pregnancy, some of my clients have shared the negative pronouncements they have heard from these same doctors, stating the unlikelihood of ever experiencing pregnancy. In my opinion, these pronouncements are like modern-day enchantments, because a woman will believe her doctor, and because the mind is so powerful, the resulting negative feelings can be counterproductive to conception, leaving women to become despondent.

Reiki calms the emotions. When she is calm, it is much easier for a woman to change her perspective and be able to draw things to a happy conclusion. Why? My practice has taught me many things, and what I have learned by working with these women is that we can call the spirit of a child when the mother-to-be is in a receptive state, which means that she is calm. A calm heart and mind "believes" in its own power to create outcomes. Time after time, I have given Reiki sessions to women in this type of situation, and I have to say that it's effective! I have a pretty good track record with helping women to get pregnant, and then seeing their pregnancies safely through to the end.

In an unusual case of this type, a friend of mine recommended that a woman named Maja come to see me to help her to conceive and carry full term. A dark-haired beauty from Venezuela, Maja was a doctor married to an American doctor. She decided to follow the recommendation and came to me because she kept having miscarriages. Maja was a scientist through and through. It was only her desperation for a child that opened her up to the possibility that Reiki might offer to her.

When I had my hands on her belly, I felt that everything was fine inside her—I could feel no distress or energy blockages at all. I asked her, "Maja, please tell me what you have been thinking about regarding your attempts to have a baby."

She sat right up, throwing the covers off her. Swinging her legs around to sit on the edge of the table, she said, "Well, I know it's all my fault that I keep having miscarriages. I never should have waited so long. My husband wanted us to have a child years ago, but I refused." Tears were welling up in her eyes as she remembered back in time. "I was so happy to be a doctor in America, where I could be a success as a woman, and it meant the world to me that I could stand up on my own and be counted." She took a huge intake of breath and then burst into tears. "But I never should have put myself first. I am being punished for being selfish!"

I was stunned by her words. "Maja, that's not true! Who told you these things?"

"My mother! My mother has been nagging me for the past five years to get pregnant, and now she yells every time I have a miscarriage, saying I will never give her a grandchild because I'm just too selfish."

People say the damnedest things, with the most horrible results.

"I hate to be the one to break it to you, Maja, but did you ever stop to think that maybe your mother doesn't know *everything*?" As I helped her to lie back down, I said, "Try to relax for now. Let's just see what we can figure out in the next hour."

Of course, being a doctor at a hospital is an exhausting profession, so Maja fell asleep almost immediately. As I stood with my hands channeling the love that is Reiki into her abdomen, I felt a brilliant light standing right next to me. It was her child, yet he seemed so emotionally mature and I could sense that he was a spiritual teacher. He said, *Please ask my mother to relax more. I need her to relax. She needs to know that I am already wishing to be born to her. Get her to accept me. Tell her I am bringing gifts to her.*

When the session was over, I decided the best time to tell Maja this news was before she was completely awake, so while she was still coming out of the Reiki experience, I held her hand and told her what had happened.

"Oh my goodness! Why would such a spiritual being choose *me* to be his mother? My life is nothing like that; I'm all about medicine and science."

"I don't know, Maja, but he wants you to relax and accept that he is your son. Can you try?"

Maja got pregnant within the month, carried her baby full term, and gave birth to a robust and healthy son. She sent word to me that he was indeed "lively," which made me chuckle to myself, because I knew then, as I know now, that there is much to look forward to with this child. He is a teacher who will bring gifts not only to Maja, but also to many others in his future.

There have been many Majas in my life, and let it suffice to say that this is work that is very prevalent for me. Yet, healing the emotions with Reiki crosses into many populations. Reiki even does a fantastic job of changing the patterns of failure resulting from messages a person may have received from their parents as a child by creating a state of inner calm. As you can see, healing the emotions crosses into many of us who make up humankind. It's really wonderful to be able to offer Reiki to those in need of emotional easefulness. The results in one's daily life are truly incredible when one is able to attain a state of inner calm.

What follows is a guided exercise that brings you into the present. By refocusing the mind and heart in the "now," emotional balance can begin to be restored. This brings a kind of inner clarity, which can bring you one step closer to understanding what Reiki has to offer.

Practicing Being Present

Being present is such a simple thing, but it's incredible how often we get caught up in the hectic pace of our daily lives and forget to take a moment to make sure we're living mindfully and enjoying the moments. That's what life is about: we're here to *experience*. Joy, laughter, sunshine, birds, a soft breeze, the taste of a freshly brewed cup of coffee—it's the simple things that can delight us when we can remember to pay attention and be in the "now." Most of the time our minds are wandering all over the place, connecting to worrisome ideas that produce unhappy emotions. We're constantly living in the past or worrying about the future. And believe me, this will always lead to unhappiness. There is no point in reliving past situations we have no power to change, or spending time inventing new endings or new beginnings to things that really don't matter in the grand scheme of things. Working with energy is a wonderful way to become happy and to transform your life into one of wonder. In order to work with energy, one must be present.

You have the power to bring yourself back to the present any time you notice that your mind is leading you on a wild-goose chase, or when you notice that you feel unhappy. At times like this, it only takes a flash of awareness to turn the whole situation around into one of enjoyment.

When you know your mind is out of control, simply notice that you are breathing. Watch yourself breathe. You breathe all the time without effort. When you watch your breathing, you always become present. You can also shift your awareness to something around you—the wind on your skin, the tree leaves rustling in the breeze, the feeling of your feet upon the earth. Where is your clothing resting on you? Is the air temperature cool, hot, or warm? If you're outside, feel the sun; notice any scents in the air, any movement of the birds or butterflies.

Any attention you pay to your sensory experiences will bring you present, which I promise will greatly increase both your happiness and your appreciation for the gift that is your life.

Sports is human life in microcosm.

—*Howard Cosell*[13]

CHAPTER 4

Healing the Body: Reiki in Professional Sports

Things took an unexpected turn as we made our way into the new millennium. My dreams remained focused on expanding my work into new areas, though I didn't have any idea of what that was going to look like. I let myself relax into waiting to see what would show up in that mystical way Reiki has of bringing things to you.

I decided to spend some time reading the old stories about alchemists while I waited. I thought those tales might hold an inkling of inspiration as to what my future might be, as some of my clients had started professing that my work was "alchemical." However, the more I read, the more I was sure that traditional alchemy didn't hold any clues. Trying to use fire for transformation? No, I don't think so—it's not me. In fact, I almost set my apartment on fire once heating up a tortilla in the toaster oven. With me being so dangerous in a modern-day laboratory called the kitchen, all my studies on the subject of alchemy brought nothing new to bear.

When the new work finally arrived, it was a total surprise. The idea to bring Reiki into the New York and national sports world came from my husband, Michael, who is a musician and composer by day and harbinger of genius ideas by night. Our son, John, now grown, was disenchanted with his career in the restaurant business. As we were sitting around the living room just chatting about what his dream job might be, he'd narrowed it down to something having to do with sports. As a youth, John's dad had helped him to grow up with the support he needed to expand his natural athletic abilities. John had always been a talented athlete who had excelled in baseball, basketball, really any sport he put his hand or foot to. He idolized professional athletes and knew everything about their stats, strengths, and weaknesses—you name it, he knew it.

"Wait a minute," Michael suddenly straightened in his chair. "What if the two of you teamed up to start a Reiki company that treated professional athletes?"

John and I looked at him as I felt a thrill go through my body. I'd been sharing my Reiki stories with John for years, and I'd even given him some treatments, so he was familiar with its benefits. With his background in sports, he instantly understood that Reiki could be immensely helpful with physical injury, from pulled muscles to fatigue to hyperextension. We looked back at each other, smiling.

It's wonderful to be a Reiki master when your son wants to become one, too. I was able to train John, and it was fun to see that he, just like all new practitioners, was excitedly amazed to feel the Reiki energy pouring through his body at ever-increasing levels as he went through the attunement processes. It was thrilling to witness him so happy to be doing what was, for him personally and for our family as a team, "the new work."

On December 21, 2000, ProReiki officially opened.

We worked on putting together brochures that were ready for mailing in February 2001, at which time we sent them to all the major northeast NFL teams: the Giants, the Ravens, the Jets, and the Eagles. Luckily for us (though sadly for us as fans), the Giants had just lost the Super Bowl to the Ravens. Unbeknown to us, the Giants were already looking for new methodologies to give them a leg up in the coming season, so when we mailed our brochure to the head coach, he passed it along to the director of player development, former Giants fullback Charles Way. Before we knew it, we had a meeting scheduled with Mr. Way out at Giants Stadium.

The night before our meeting, a blizzard dumped two feet of snow over the tri-state area. As the lone taxi we flagged down navigated the treacherous New York City streets, John watched the snowy world pass by from the window of the car, his brilliant blue eyes contemplative. Here it was, already March of 2001 and Reiki was not being used in the sports world at all. Given the incredible healing of physical injuries I'd seen with clients in private practice, it seemed ridiculous that the people who relied on their bodies most had never even heard of it.

As we drove, John fed me background knowledge on Charles "Get Out of My" Way (this had me in stitches), and his five successful seasons as a fullback for the New York Giants. Now, as director of player development, he'd agreed to our meeting to better understand how Reiki could help players as they went through the rigors of a career in professional football.

We relinquished what was very likely the only operating taxi in all of New York City and the cold winter air bit at us as we made our way through the snow-covered Meadowlands parking lot, pausing for a moment at the glass double doors. A security guard led us through the locked front door of the business offices. Photos from past games plastered the walls thick as wallpaper, and behind a pristine glass cabinet was a glistening Super Bowl trophy from ten years prior.

Young, handsome, and soft-spoken with a wide, beautiful smile, Charles Way struck me right away as a real gentleman. We followed his hulking frame down a hallway and into a conference room, where once settled, Charles launched right in. "Okay, so here we are. Tell me about this Reiki. Is it religious? Because I'm not interested in anything that goes against my Christian faith." I stressed that Reiki has nothing to do with any religion or belief system. This put him at ease and he was totally comfortable about continuing our conversation.

"Okay, I'm glad to get that cleared up," he said, raising his eyebrows. "Now tell me why the New York Giants should use Reiki as part of what we offer our players?"

"Well," John began, leaning across the wide table, "Reiki is one of the best techniques to help prevent and treat injuries. We can use it on the guys to help quicken the healing process for everything from a pulled hamstring to a concussion. It can help reenergize the team after tough workouts, which," he grinned, "actually helps to prevent injuries due to muscle exertion."

"Go on," Charles waited.

"And for any injured players, Reiki can also lessen the pain they're experiencing, allowing them to get back on the field more quickly. We've had client cases where a few Reiki treatments have eliminated pain altogether."

Charles nodded, considering it all before telling us his own story. An all-star player for the Giants, he'd destroyed his knee in 1999. Despite the fact that he'd blown his knee, he continued to play, scoring multiple touchdowns and setting records for yards rushing. He had wanted to delay what he knew was inevitable surgery. Since then, he'd undergone three major operations in an attempt to fix it, all to no avail. He even made medical history when, on December 15, 1999, he'd had the cartilage in his right knee replaced with the cartilage of a cadaver. It was the first operation of its kind for an athlete, and regrettably, it failed. Worse, they had to open his knee back up to remove that cartilage in yet another operation.

After so many failed operations, his knee finally forced him into early retirement. Looking weary from remembering, he folded his hands and looked at us squarely across the table. "I'll tell you what. I'll be the guinea pig," he shrugged. "If this Reiki stuff works on me, then I'll look into bringing you onboard for the team."

"All right," I smiled, "we'll take that bet." Getting up from the table, he raised his pants leg to show us what we were working with. Though it had been two years since his last surgery, his knee was still extremely swollen. He confided that it was painful just to walk, especially on busy game days when he had to be out on the field, moving constantly between the players as an encouraging support to them on the sidelines. Deciding that no one would likely be around due to the bad weather, Charles offered to take us into the Giants' locker room so we could do the session right away. It felt surreal as we wound through a maze of hallways that I never imagined I would get to see. Finally arriving at the locker room, I spotted a huge metal bathtub.

"What's that for?" I asked Charles. It looked like some sort of medieval torture device.

"Oh, that? They pack it with ice. Guys sit in there to numb pain and keep the swelling down after playing on Sundays."

The sight of it shocked me to the core. Who knew that players had to sit in there, packed in ice, following games, just to ease their suffering? One of my personal gifts kicked in. I could feel the energy of self-discipline and a wild kind of joy, mixed with pain, radiating off the athletic equipment filling the room that was used to build athletes into champions. I could feel all the lingering emotions of the New York Giants seeping into me. Suddenly I could understand something deep inside my emotional skin about what it meant to be one of them—the thrill of it all and the reasoning behind why these young men would put themselves in regular situations where injuries could cause permanent changes and pains in their bodies. I believe this understanding helped me as I went along on the path that was forming itself beneath our feet.

We put the massage table up and a very skeptical Charles stretched out on it. John and I got down to business, working on him simultaneously. Everything was going along normally until I reached his injured knee. As my hands hovered over his kneecap, I listened, and man, did it talk.

Should I really tell him? I asked my spirit guides. With so much on the line, I wasn't sure how open a major NFL player would be to hearing that I get messages from people's body parts ... not to mention spiritual beings! Who knew how he would take what I had "heard"? But the answer came right away.

Yes!

After the session was over, Charles was glowing; I knew the Reiki had done him wonders.

Taking a deep breath, I told him, "Here's the thing, Charles. Your knee is responding to the desires of a woman in your life. It stays in this condition because she doesn't want you to play football."

The look of shock on his face told me I was right even before he spoke.

"Yes," he said, carefully. "That's true. There is a woman in my life who doesn't want me to play." I didn't want to pry, so we let it go at that. But perhaps it was my knowing this that convinced him we could offer something highly unusual, something that worked on levels he simply hadn't explored yet.

By the time our session ended, a trainer and another injured player had arrived. The injured player was an offensive tackle with his arm in a sling, fresh from a shoulder surgery. As he perched on the edge of the trainer's desk, discussing the operation, Charles explained to us quietly that injured players always try to stick it out for the duration of the season, suspending their surgeries until the off-season like he'd done. What went unsaid was the fact that this practice of continuing to push through and play while injured often makes the injury much worse.

"Hey, man," Charles called from across the room. "Why don't you come over here and let these guys take a look at you." As we explained what Reiki was and why we were there, the injured player's smirk communicated his thoughts about our profession, but he nonetheless lay down on the table. His body accepted as much Reiki as John and I could dish out. Afterward, he sat up slowly, in a bit of a daze.

"Wow. Uh, that was incredible," he said gruffly. "That pain in my shoulder? It's totally gone." Then, lowering his voice so his trainer wouldn't hear, he murmured, "I think I could feel that energy you were talking about too. It actually felt pretty cool."

I never worked on that player again, but I followed his career with great interest. He went on to have two glowing seasons with the Giants before joining another NFL team in 2003. His trainer, on the other hand, was very standoffish—he'd stood with his arms crossed, watching us from across the room with unveiled distrust mingled with amusement. Because we didn't appear to be physically manipulating anything, I think it was hard for him to believe that what we were providing could possibly do any good.

Charles walked us out and shook our hands at the door. Leaning in, he said, "I'd like to come in for another treatment next week."

"Okay, uh, that's great." I managed. As soon as the door closed, John and I erupted in excitement: we had our first official NFL client.

By his third session at our office, Charles had his routine established; he hopped up on the table and fell instantly asleep in response to Reiki's power to create relaxation. In this particular session, John was working on his bad knee while I gave Reiki to his kidneys. Suddenly we were startled by a loud crack, so loud the drawers in my nearby cabinet rattled. John and I looked at each other in alarm. It was Charles's knee! We glanced at him, expecting him to come out of his Reiki-induced slumber from the sheer sound of it, but he didn't stir. I shrugged and we continued working. I'd never experienced anything like this before.

After that session, the swelling in Charles' knee disappeared. He called to tell us that he was free of pain for the first time in over two years. He began doing football drills again, as well as running and working out hard at the gym. When he arrived for his next session, his muscles had developed so quickly that we could see the physical results of all his hard work the minute he walked through the door. We couldn't help but grin.

Charles had two more Reiki sessions with us before going to see a top orthopedic surgeon who specialized in treating professional athletes... and that was when Charles was officially cleared to play football again. It was a miracle! His career-ending injury had been reversed with the help of healing Reiki.

While Charles was deciding whether or not he wanted to play for the Philadelphia Eagles, he became an advocate for us with the New York Giants. I have some really wonderful e-mails I got from Dr. Oz in those days, wishing me success in my quest to bring Reiki to professional sports. He even gave me a signed copy of his book to give to one of the coaches who invited John and me out to the stadium so he could try Reiki.

Although the trainer we'd met on our first day there was still very resistant to the idea of Reiki in the locker room, players started showing up in our office. We weren't quite sure if they were being sent, or if they were coming of their own volition due to the fact that Charles's knee had had such a miraculous recovery.

One player came our way after suffering a hamstring injury in practice. Next to injured knees, hamstrings can be one of the most dangerous body parts to harm. Once a hamstring has an injury, the injury is likely to reoccur, and it can take players out of the game indefinitely. Even though this Giants' player had a shorter-than-usual appointment, he was healed enough to play in Sunday's game. Not only that, he didn't miss a game the rest of the season and for years following.

For another player who came to us, physical injury wasn't the issue. He came our way to get our help in coping with the terrible emotional difficulties with which he was dealing. The pressure to score points had really beaten him up mentally. He tortured himself by replaying events in his head, working himself up to such a place of stress and dysfunction that he was having problems even driving his car. His emotional and mental states were so interwoven with his ability to perform physically that John and I decided to give him a combination of Reiki and hypnotherapy. This guy arrived for his sessions so stressed out he could barely lay still on the table.

He provided us the words that helped him to create positive imagery: "I have nerves of steel. I am in complete control of every muscle in my body ... I win games, baby." John and I began with the Reiki to relax him to the point of semi-sleep before beginning the hypnotherapy. He left feeling happy, healthy, confident, and strong. And each time he came for a session, his name would be in the papers the following Monday, proclaiming he'd been instrumental in another Giants' win on Sunday.

Though Reiki had made his return to football a reality, Charles Way called to tell me he had made a different decision. Expressing his deep gratitude to John and me for making it possible for him to play again, he explained that knowing he could return had freed him up to clearly look at his life and decide what he really wanted out of it. He explained that he realized if he went back to playing football, it was inevitable that another injury would come his way. Something would end his career sooner or later. His love for the game—and for the Giants—was bigger than his desire to play, so he decided to keep his post as director of player development.

Ultimately, the trainer we encountered that winter day in Giants Stadium was a gatekeeper who kept us from working with the Giants in a more extensive capacity. We couldn't fault him for it; it had to be hard for him to accept something that seemed so foreign. But the incredible support from Charles had provided us with formerly skeptical clients who now could add Reiki to their treatment options. In the big picture, I truly believe that as time goes by and we learn more about the scientific and statistical benefits of Reiki, it will flourish in professional sports. One day, thanks to Charles Way, all athletes will have the same access to Reiki masters as they do to medical doctors. Of this I have no doubt.

So, just like always, one thing leads to another, and working with the NFL opened the doors to some of the members of the NBA. Through what I like to call "the ways and means committee of the universe"—i.e., all the things we consider to be coincidences (not!) or chance fortuitous meetings (I don't think so!)—a client of mine introduced me to a woman named Carolyn Parello who had just left a position as a journalist for the NBA. Carolyn, sassy and smart, gave up her illustrious employment in the world of superstar athletes in order to pursue her heart's true desire: a career in art. When I asked Carolyn if she would like to experience Reiki and possibly recommend it to her former NBA colleagues, she was game and decided to take advantage of my offer.

Her dark hair spread out across the pillow as Carolyn came slowly awake on my table, still dreamy from her Reiki session. Based on what she had told me, I knew for a fact she was an important person to have brought into the Reiki fold. She confided that while working for the NBA, many of the players had turned to her when they had problems and considered her help to be big "medicine" for their most important concerns. Star athletes are isolated from the general public to a large degree, and to those who guard their privacy, their being kept apart from fans is for their own good. Professional athletes are constantly chased after by unscrupulous people—everyone from gold diggers to crooked investment bankers has them in their sights. Carolyn was a buffer for professional athletes; she was someone for them to befriend who was not only a member of regular society, but also wise, kind, and even genuinely sweet.

With her eyes still slits full of Reiki wonder, she softly explained, "The NBA is huge and slow to move, but I can see this would help the players."

With Carolyn's help, John and I were invited to an event where we gave sessions to current and retired players. Although some of the retired guys were in the Hall of Fame, no amount of recognition could make up for the physical pain their bodies were in due to a former career in basketball.

The first person to come in arrived in a red polo shirt and loose khakis, looking to be in great pain. He lay down on the table with his forehead puckered in a grimace. "I have a headache so bad I can hardly see," he told me. He went on to explain that his chronic neck pain caused frequent unbearable headaches. "I've got real problems from all the times I snapped my head back making jump shots."

He told us that his time was limited, so John and I worked on him together for approximately twenty minutes. When we were done, his reaction was astounding. "I can't believe it," he enthused, moving his head from side to side. "All the pain in my neck and head is gone! This is a miracle!"

"Miracle" was the word we heard over and over again as we addressed painful knees, hips, backs, ankles, necks, and wrists. Every single player we gave Reiki to loved it, and word spread. All this talk of "miracles" brought a particularly interesting man to us who was skeptical to the point of being confrontational. I knew it was because he was suffering from unbearable pain from old injuries, but it still stunned me to be talked to so harshly by a complete stranger. He was very handsome and arrived dressed impeccably, leaning on a cane. The constant pain in his hip was beginning to really wear him down, causing a bad temper.

"I don't believe in this for one minute," he snarled at me, "I'm here to disprove what everybody wants so desperately to believe about you two, and I'm going to save all these friends of mine from their delusions!" I know my eyes must have widened with shock, as he started climbing up on to the table, continuing to say, "I've been to every doctor there is, and I know you can't help me. You're going to fail, and I'm going to tell you right to your faces 'I told you so' before I leave this room to go save my friends from such charlatans!" He thrashed around on the table, clenching his teeth and muttering a bunch of expletives. He had worked himself up into quite a rage.

Without saying a word, John and I looked at each other and got down to the business of addressing the situation. This man had come with his challenge at the end of a long day, and even though we had officially closed down for the night, we still gave him Reiki in a session so powerful we lost track of time. Our concentration was almost exclusively on his hips. Both hips were in dire need of attention, and they absorbed Reiki in torrents that were practically overwhelming in strength. This is because if one side of the body has an injury, the other side becomes exhausted and worn down from picking up the slack for the other side. When he sat up, he was quite groggy, but at least he was no longer angry.

Beginning to climb down off the table, he almost fell, crying out, "Oh, my God, I can't stand up!" John caught him as he was falling. The man's eyes were filling up with tears that he didn't want us to see.

Was this man's apparent "bad reaction" to Reiki unusual? No, not really. Reiki always brings things to a head, although we can't predict exactly what that is going to look like. This was an old injury, and an injury that had been compounded over time. There was a history of this retired player reinjuring his hip over and over again while he had been an active player, so his hip was never given the opportunity to heal in the first place. Reiki had awakened the original deep wound, which is called a "healing crisis." When this occurs, the pain can get worse before it gets better. Another result from a Reiki session can be that the pain continues to worsen while the person with the injury finds they suddenly have the inner strength to take the action necessary to really address the issue—such as getting a hip replacement to get rid of pain once and for all.

Jumping back to our session, we had no idea how this was going to play out. Straightening and turning to look into John's face, with his voice full of pain, the man whispered, "What should I do now, John?" He was gingerly testing his ability to stand on his own, and spoke louder, with returning anger, "I told you that you couldn't help me!" He was starting to fume. With John's assistance, he hobbled to the door, where he had left his cane propped against its frame.

"Listen, it might get better overnight," John told him calmly. "Try to get some sleep, and if it still hurts in the morning, come back first thing."

With that, we all went out into the hallway. I closed the door behind us on what had been a very intense but interesting day, to say the very least. We were staying in the conference center's hotel, and as we made our way down the hall to our rooms, I felt grateful that John and I could move with ease, while watching that poor man suffer his way slowly.

When we arrived in the dining room for breakfast the next morning, we saw the retired player from the night before sitting at a table, talking animatedly and looking all around. When he saw us, he literally jumped up and *ran* to us, sans cane.

"Hey, I don't know what in the world you did, but I woke up this morning for the first time in years without any pain!" He clapped first John and then me on the back, smiling from ear to ear. "I want everybody to know about this Reiki stuff! I'm really sorry I was so grouchy last night but hey, I'm making up for it now, aren't I, by being such a great advertisement?" With that, he grabbed John and me in a group hug, right there in the dining room in front of a whole league of current and retired professional athletes. No better advertisement, indeed!

By the time John and I had to leave to go back to New York City, guys were lined up outside our door, asking us, "Please, could you just give me five minutes of Reiki?" They were all returning home, and they all wanted a little hit of Reiki for the ride.

Although we enjoyed our time working with professional athletes, the urge to keep pushing forward into the world of sports began to fade in the face of the many everyday people who daily stood in line outside the door of my office, waiting for Reiki. These were the people who really wanted it. In that light, we turned our focus back to our regular clientele.

The secret of the care of the patient
is in caring for the patient.
—*Francis W. Peabody,*
Harvard University 1925[14]

CHAPTER 5

Using Reiki in Cancer Treatment

After more than ten years had passed since I went into the operating room with Susanna and Dr. Oz, I was unexpectedly brought into the medical world again. In August of 2010, a beautiful young lady in her early twenties came to my office on a sunny afternoon. Wendy knew about Reiki and had decided to avail herself of it in order to help her cope with the overwhelming and devastating news her doctor had delivered a few days prior. She had just been told she had a malignant tumor in her right breast.

Wendy's emotional state was so extreme that I needed to self-protect as best I could in order to be of service to her. In order to establish a bit of emotional distance, I simply called to my Reiki master in spirit, asking to be filled with pure love as I listened to Wendy expressing her anguish. My heart swelled with love for her while I focused on how the sunlight shining through my office window was creating a halo effect around her hair as she sobbed. I concentrated on how celestial she appeared, which was in stark contrast to the extraordinary depths of her personal hell. "Raven, I am absolutely terrified," she cried. "I just don't know how I'm going to be able to handle this. I have so many dreams for my life that just won't come true if I lose my breast!"

I had no words with which to comfort her. As I handed her tissues and held her hand while she cried, the only thing I knew for certain was that Reiki would help her deal with her emotions. When her sobs began to subside, I looked directly into her eyes. "Okay, Wendy, I know this is really, really tough. But let's see how we can manage by facing up to it together and doing our best." With that, she lay down on the soft green sheets of my massage table. I covered her with a blanket, hoping that maybe, just maybe, she would feel safe, even if it was just for a little while.

I rubbed my hands together, summoning Reiki into my palms, and silently prayed, *I ask to be hollow and to fill with unconditional love. I open to receive the blessings of Reiki.*

As I placed my hands over her midsection, energy jolted through me in response to Wendy's deep need. Although we can never predict what the results of Reiki's presence will be, as waves of beautiful healing light poured through my body and out my hands into Wendy, her tears quickly stopped. I could feel the Reiki flowing through me at a rapid rate of speed while her breathing slowed down. Within minutes, I felt her body shift into deep relaxation, and in no time at all, she was sound asleep.

As Wendy slowly sat up at the end of the session, she began to speak. Looking at me with eyes full of wonder, she softly proclaimed, "Raven, I think this is happening to me for a reason. I can't figure out what the reason is yet, but I don't feel like a victim anymore. I think something good is going to come out of this. I just can't see what it is yet—I can only feel it coming."

I felt victory with a capital V! From my point of view, we had just won a major battle. She climbed down off the table and sat in my cushy white chair, where I handed her a glass of water. After finishing the water, she was fully awake. We made another appointment and with a final hug, I sent her on her way.

Although our intention initially was to address Wendy's fears while she interviewed surgeons, things took an unexpected turn. Within a week's time, Wendy came to her third Reiki session with a big announcement to make: she had decided to engage Dr. Sheldon Marc Feldman, Chief of Breast Surgery at New York-Columbia Presbyterian Hospital, to perform the surgery her oncologist recommended. Her eyes were shining with happiness as she bubbled over with excitement. "Oh, Raven, I'm so relieved! Dr. Feldman says you can come into the operating room with me!"

I sat motionless, very aware of how I kept my face completely still as she continued to happily express all the wonderful things she felt about Dr. Feldman. Meanwhile, inside I felt incredible and familiar turmoil. *Oh, geez!* I was thinking to myself. *I wasn't expecting to do* that *again—go back into that scary place full of all that terrifying equipment?* But how could I disappoint her? I could see she felt braver just talking about my being there. I knew she really needed my support, so I told myself, *Listen, you just have to buck up and be strong. Another woman needs you, and you just can't let her down!*

Further tests confirmed that Wendy's tumor was rather large, and it was surrounded by other smaller tumors that might or might not be malignant. She told me of the frantic conversations she began to have with Dr. Feldman in which she pleaded with him to tell her of any possible way around losing her breast. After looking at all the test results and gauging their probable meaning, Dr. Feldman agreed that she could keep her breast if the other tumors were benign and, most importantly, if her lymph nodes were clear. None of these things would be known until he removed everything during the surgery and got the pathology report from the hospital's lab delivered to him right there in the operating room. This meant that the final decision would be made while she was under anesthesia and she wouldn't know whether she was able to keep her breast until she awoke.

Wendy and I had several Reiki sessions in the two weeks prior to surgery, concentrating on seeing her lymph nodes clear and the other tumors benign. It was a very big deal to us both when another test about a week before her surgery showed that her tumor had shrunk in size! Wendy began to feel much more confident with each passing day. She started having profound dreams at night in which she saw herself helping women in the future.

On the morning of her surgery, the sun was just rising as I came up from the underground subway station. I made note of the birds singing in the trees along West 168th Street. *A good sign?* I wondered. Grabbing a cup of coffee from a vendor's truck, I gulped it down while rushing along the street toward the hospital to meet Wendy. When I joined her on the third floor of the

Millstein Building at Columbia Presbyterian, she was shaking with nerves.

After checking in, we were escorted by intake nurses to the pre-op area. Other doctors on the surgery team introduced themselves to her while technicians and nurses readied her for the operating room. We were surrounded by a flurry of activity, with each new person asking Wendy countless questions, many of them repeats, writing down her answers on official forms: "What is your name?" "What is your date of birth?" "Why are you here?" and "Which breast is it?" I held Wendy's hand through it all, sending little blasts of Reiki into her palm whenever appropriate. As the anesthesiologist was speaking with her, I felt a sudden skip in my heart when Wendy cried out with relief in her voice, "Oh, here comes Dr. Feldman!" I looked up to see a striking man with salt-and-pepper hair and intent brown eyes dressed in blue scrubs under a white lab coat. This was the man who was about to change both of our lives forever.

"How do you do, Raven," he said, putting out his hand for me to shake at Wendy's introduction. "Sorry to rush you along, but here are your scrubs. Could you please put these on right away? I want you to go to radiology with Wendy, and they're waiting for her now." He pointed toward the restroom, where I was obviously meant to change. Once the door closed behind me, I took in a long slow breath, noticing how shaky

I felt inside. Looking in the mirror, I allowed myself to acknowledge how nervous I really was and began some serious self-talk. Looking into my own eyes, I thought to myself, *The only way out is through. Be strong. Wendy needs you.* And to my guides, while changing into the scrubs, *I ask to be a pure vessel for Reiki. I call to my Reiki master in spirit to be with me now, and I thank you from the bottom of my heart for your assistance.*

Emerging from the restroom dressed in blue from head to toe, booties now covered my shoes and a blue net was over my hair. A nurse took my street clothes and purse, putting everything into a locker. As Dr. Feldman walked Wendy and me through the maze of hallways, he was exuding confidence and warmly expressed how happy he was that Wendy had me with her. When we got to radiology, he pushed open the door and introduced us to Dr. Higgins, explaining to her that he wanted me to give Reiki to Wendy as much as was possible and appropriate during the needle localization procedure. Leaving us in her charge, Dr. Feldman sped back down the hall with, "Thank you, Dr. Higgins!" ringing out behind him.

We were taken to a tiny room full of equipment with a transparent shield in one corner. Dr. Higgins was just as surprised as I was at my being there. However, she seemed very happy to have me. "Well, I don't know what Reiki is, but if it can help Wendy now, that's all that matters to me." The technologist slipped the gown off Wendy's shoulders and turned her toward the breast-imaging machine, getting everything ready to take an x-ray. Every woman of a certain age knows what the pressing of a mammogram is like. "Don't move or breathe," Dr. Higgins said to Wendy, pulling me behind the shield where she was reviewing the images on the monitor. In a millisecond, the first x-ray of Wendy's breast was taken. "Okay, Wendy, you can breathe now." Next, Dr. Higgins asked me to apply Reiki directly into Wendy's back while she inserted a hollow needle into Wendy's flattened breast. The needle had a wire inside it that would lead Dr. Feldman to the tumor.

Wendy was completely awake for this painful process. It was shocking for me to witness, to say the least, but I couldn't think about that now. My only job was to maintain the flow of Reiki so it could lend strength to Wendy. I felt overflowing concern for Dr. Higgins and Wendy both; they were locked in the drama of doctor and patient, each reacting accordingly, Dr. Higgins with compassion and Wendy with unavoidable pain. My role with Reiki was to help Wendy to endure the pain. Another x-ray was taken to make sure the wire did in fact lead to the exact location of the tumor. Next the hollow needle was removed, leaving the wire behind as the guide for Dr. Feldman to follow.

This stressful and painful procedure was repeated five times, as Wendy had five tumors. While behind the shield during one of the x-rays, Dr. Higgins told me she was very glad that I was there to bring relief to Wendy, because this was the first and only time she had ever been asked to insert five wires. I could feel how sorry she was that she had to do something so painful, yet so necessary, if Wendy was to have any chance of keeping her breast. I wondered to myself, *How do women go through this without Reiki? How do they manage it?*

My presence was a shock in the operating room to most of the surgery team. "Why are you here?" "What are you doing?" I was being asked while I sat on a stool at the end of the operating table, my place for the surgery. As I began to channel Reiki into the top of Wendy's head, at Dr. Feldman's encouragement, I answered the questions posed to me, giving doctors and nurses what I hoped was a suitable crash course in Reiki. "I'm sending healing energy out of my hands and in through the top of Wendy's head. This energy called Reiki is traveling though her body to assist in healing while the operation is in progress." While answering questions, I had to look up and saw things I didn't wish to see. Not only that, I felt like the glaring lights were burning into my mind and soul. Once everyone was focused in on the operation and too busy to ask me further questions, I crouched down on the stool next to the anesthesiologist and continued to send Reiki directly into the top of Wendy's head. I closed my eyes. Dr. Feldman's voice was calling out for instruments.

Every now and then, Dr. Feldman would ask, "How's she doing, Raven?"

"Fine!" I would answer, my eyes remaining closed. I didn't need my eyes to tell me the answer. I could feel Wendy absorbing Reiki beautifully in a constant, uninterrupted flow.

After a while, one of the young doctors asked me another question. *Oh my goodness!* I thought to myself in shock as I looked up to answer. It was in that split second of raising my eyes that I saw way too clearly what was happening to Wendy. I felt a wave of nausea hit my stomach.

Breathe! I heard my inner voice say. With that, I took a deep breath, quickly answered the question, and scooted down even lower on the stool. Closing my eyes tightly, I began to pretend that I was in a fairytale land filled with love and peace and laughter. Wendy and I were in a faerie bower, with a gently tinkling brook running by and a breeze filled with the scent of flowers. Reiki poured through me and into Wendy as the scene changed. Now we were floating together on a cloud in the presence of Archangel Gabriel. Angels surrounded us, singing. I listened to them as they sang us all the way back to the feelings of safety and serenity that dwell in my office. Time stood still.

All of a sudden, there was a phone ringing somewhere in the distance. The sound jarred me back to the operating room, and I knew this was it. This was the crucial moment. My eyes flew open. Dr. Feldman had promised Wendy that no negative conversation would be allowed in the operating room during her surgery, so in case the report was not positive, he would not take the news on speakerphone. Being scrubbed and gloved, he couldn't touch the phone, so he asked the head OR nurse to hold the receiver up to his ear. "Oh, thank you!" and then to the room, "Team, no surprises. The pathology on her lymph nodes is negative. Everything's clear. We're closing up." Wendy was going to be keeping her breast! They were all so happy.

As for me, I could have cheered out loud right then and there, but instead, I curled down even more on the stool while turning my head away so no one could see the tears in my eyes. I thanked every good thing in the universe for this happy outcome and for the wild joy I felt in my heart, created by Dr. Feldman's incredible surgical skills ... and by his embracing of Reiki.

A new phase was beginning for me as well as for Reiki. Dr. Feldman called to ask if I would consider working with his future patients who were open to it and could afford to pay for my services.

Dr. Feldman's patients began to arrive at my office.

The first to come was Tansy, who was just past her thirtieth birthday. Tansy didn't actually have cancer, but she did have a predisposition for it. Her grandmother, all of her aunts, and her mother had succumbed to breast cancer. It had taken her the seven years since her mother's death to face getting a bilateral mastectomy in order to prevent the loss of her own life. She cried inconsolably on my massage table. For all the years since her mother's death, Dr. Feldman had been telling her that she needed to get this done. Tansy was a devotee of Yoga and ate only organic foods. Dr. Feldman had informed her that even if she did Yoga every single day and never ate a vegetable grown within one hundred miles of a pesticide, it was unlikely to make a difference.

I held her in my arms as if she were my own child, her brown curls pressed up against my shoulder while her sobs became more intense. All I could do was hold on to her as she wept bitterly, soaking me with tears. As with Wendy, there was nothing I could say to make it better. What do you say to someone young and unmarried who had always wanted to nurse her babies one day?

When her sobs finally subsided, I laid her down on the pink sheets and covered her with a fuzzy green blanket. As this powerful session began, I felt beautiful spirits moving around her, including her own mother, but I didn't say anything about that for fear she would start crying again. The Reiki poured through at a very high level. Tansy fell into a deep sleep and woke up feeling peaceful. She left my office feeling much more accepting of what was before her.

I didn't see Tansy again until the morning of her surgery. I arrived ahead of her, as did her family. With the sun beginning to shine brightly through the atrium windows of the Milstein Hospital Building, her stepmother tearfully confided, "Raven, I feel you should know this in case you can do something about it. Tansy is absolutely terrified she is going to wake up after the surgery with so many regrets she will be unable to face the rest of her life."

I didn't know what to say. "I'll pray to the spirits to help her," was all I could manage.

Once in pre-op, all the usual things were happening for the first hour. Tansy was reclining on the pre-op bed in her gown, blue hair net, and hospital booties to keep her feet warm. Of course, I gave her as much Reiki as I could while she was answering the seemingly never-ending questions posed to her by doctors, nurses, and technicians.

As I was about to find out, there is a certain kind of pain management procedure that requires a pre-operative insertion. The anesthesiologist came in to ask, "Tansy, do you want to have a pain block inserted into your back?"

"Why? What's it for?"

"It helps with the pain for tomorrow."

"Oh, I don't know. Raven, do you think I should?"

"I can't tell you, darling."

"Okay, I'll do it. Now I want everybody out of here! I just want to be with Raven!"

Everyone left, and the departing nurse pulled the curtains around us. I held Tansy's hand as she started to cry.

"Raven, what am I doing? My breasts haven't done anything wrong, and here I am, about to get mutilated. What am I doing?" she folded in upon herself with tears and gut-wrenching sobs.

From some ancient place inside, I knew exactly what to do.

"Tansy, you're doing this to save your own life! Let's have a ceremony to say good-bye to your breasts. We'll make it so they understand, okay? Take my hands and close your eyes."

Together, we began to pray. I called to the highest of spiritual beings from the highest of spiritual realms to create a circle of pure light and unconditional love around Tansy and me. I called to the Great Mother Goddess and to Tansy's own mother to join us inside the circle. At my instructions, Tansy spoke directly to her breasts, repeating after me, "Thank you for everything you have given to me. I am not mad at you. I love you very much and I send you into the light for safekeeping. I am sending you into everything that is sacred and holy. Please dwell forever in the eternal light that is love.

Thank you, and good-bye. I bless you, bless you, bless you."

As soon as we were done with the ceremony, it was time to go to the OR for the insertion of the pain block she had agreed to. They gave her a light sedative, but she had to be awake for it. I stayed at her feet, giving her Reiki through the bottoms of her feet, but the fact is, it was very painful for her to have the two ports inserted on either side of her upper spine. As the procedure progressed, she cried out, "RAVEN!" at a point when the pain was really bad.

"I'm right here, sweetheart—I'm right here, sending Reiki through your feet." She was crying and I felt so bad for her.

After that, everything went smoothly during the bilateral mastectomy, which was followed immediately by the beginning phases of reconstructive plastic surgery. The chief of the plastic surgery team was stunned that I was there and asked me plenty of questions. By the end of the surgery, I was surprised, because he seemed to be very interested in what I was doing and asked for my card (which I didn't have, since all my things were with Tansy's parents in the waiting room).

The real blessing came when Tansy was waking up on the operating table. "Tansy, you did great! You were great!" I enthused to her, while holding her hand tightly.

"Is it over?" she asked groggily, "Aren't we on the beach? Am I in Hawaii?" As a little grin split her face, she looked into my eyes, "I never felt better in my life. Oh, thank you, thank you so much!" She began to smile in earnest, and became radiant. It was the talk of the hospital the next day.

Tansy never felt sad following the surgery. To this day, she continues to do very well indeed, looking forward to the beautiful life that lies before her, instead of always looking over her shoulder with worry about breast cancer.

Breast cancer. Striking women and men of every age. Putting them in positions where they need to make really tough choices.

Like Alysha, in her late thirties, who chose to have a bilateral mastectomy, even though she had cancer in only one breast. "Why take chances?" she told me. And anyway, she would have to have plastic surgery on the healthy breast later. Might as well get everything done at once, right? In her case, Alysha's insurance company had reneged on paying for one of the more expensive procedures she needed, so she didn't have any extra money for Reiki. But Dr. Feldman really wanted her to have it, so her extended family chipped in to pay for my services.

I was with Alysha in pre-op when Dr. Feldman had the final conversation with her about whether or not she should have a port put in to accommodate the upcoming chemotherapy she would need after surgery.

"It's entirely up to you, Alysha, I don't have a preference as to whether you get the port put in, or not. You can also get the chemo through an IV each time you go for your treatments."

I gave her Reiki through the bottoms of her feet as the conversation continued.

"I just want you to know that sometimes the port will go in easily, and sometimes it's a struggle to get it in."

"I've decided to have the port put in, please," she said in a soft voice to Dr. Feldman. "I just hate needles."

When it came time to put the port in during surgery, Dr. Feldman selected a place in her upper chest. "Well, this looks like a good vein," he said to the surgery team. Knowing his concerns, I was extra careful to move my thinking mind out of the way in order to become hollow so that Reiki could pour through me like gangbusters. In the next moment, Dr. Feldman whispered to me, "Thanks, Raven, it went right in."

In modern medicine today, a woman has choices to make when she gets breast cancer surgery. I was called in on a case for someone who was receiving a new type of reconstructive surgery following the removal of one breast. In this procedure, fat is taken from the woman's abdomen to build a breast from her own tissue, rather than having the type of reconstructive surgery that requires an implant. This makes for a very long day in the OR.

Dr. Feldman really wanted Theresa to have Reiki, especially because her surgery was going to be more complicated than usual. She called me just to be able to tell Dr. Feldman that she had contacted me, but the truth was she had no extra money available to her with which to pay for Reiki. In our initial conversation, I told her about Alysha's family and how they had chipped in for her, which inspired Theresa to e-mail her many friends, asking for twenty-dollar donations so she could have the Reiki Dr. Feldman had recommended.

The money poured in.

I knew from the start that the surgery was going to take much longer than I could handle on my own. The normal time for a surgery can be anywhere from four to six hours, even for something relatively easy. In this case, the prediction was that the surgery would last nine to twelve hours, and I was aware of what that would mean for me. You see, once the commitment is made to go to surgery, I don't leave the patient alone in the OR for longer than it takes to get a quick sip of water or to use the restroom when necessary. "Out and quickly back" is the name of the game when you are the Reiki master responsible for providing healing energy. The idea of staying in there for twelve hours without a real break was overwhelming and I knew I couldn't do it.

John and I made a plan of how we could help Theresa by working the case together. We were both there for her first Reiki session so that she could meet us and begin to establish a strong connection to us both. She had two more Reiki sessions in the two weeks before her surgery, one with me and one with John. This worked like a charm; we three became a solid working unit.

As prearranged, on the morning of Theresa's surgery, John and I met Dr. Feldman at 6:30 a.m. in his office to pick up our scrubs. The entire breast cancer floor was dark, except for Dr. Feldman's office. He was the only one already at work. His comment about the chemotherapy port during Alysha's surgery had piqued my interest, so while he fished our scrubs out of the hall closet, I asked him, "Dr. Feldman, do you feel the Reiki in the operating room? Can you feel a difference when the patient is getting Reiki?"

"Oh, yes, Raven, I can. I think everyone feels it, but they just don't know what it is." He didn't comment further as he handed over the scrubs and hurried back down the hall to his endless paperwork and all the details he needed to address before the upcoming surgery. His quick answer to my questions gave me the chills, but deep down inside, I wasn't totally surprised. For example, when I'm teaching Reiki and demonstrating how to perform a Reiki session on a volunteer, everyone in the room feels its power, even though they are not on the table receiving the treatment.

When Theresa's surgery began, I was the one with her in the OR. Two surgery teams worked together simultaneously, and this meant there were seventeen people standing around her as she lay on the operating table. Operating rooms aren't very big, and this was a real crowd! Theresa's plastic surgeon was there from the very beginning, doing microsurgery on her stomach all during Dr. Feldman's part of the breast removal.

I stayed for the first part of the operation, and then John relieved me. About eleven hours after the surgery began, the plastic surgeon was finally sewing veins and blood vessels back together, while everyone watched on a screen overhead. John was very excited as he reported to me, "I never saw anything like that in my life!" With true awe in his voice, he continued, "That surgeon rocks!" It was a long and harrowing day but everything was a total success. I got chills as John described how the doctor was sewing with needles so small they were practically invisible to the naked eye, and it wasn't an easy job to do. Tiny pieces of veins were slipping out of the stitches as she sewed. It was so stressful that at one point she had cried out, "John! I think I need some Reiki! Can you direct some to me?" She was an intrepid surgeon. She had been there the entire time, looking through glasses with microscopes attached to them.

In one case, a young patient of Dr. Feldman's who needed a lumpectomy had parents who were very nervous and fearful—more than most parents. This was when I discovered for the first time that it is wise to share Reiki with family members, as is appropriate, on the day of surgery. The help I gave to her parents by simply taking just a few moments between things produced amazing benefits. This has now become standard procedure for me if the family members and their spirits are willing.

The healing I needed for myself in order to be comfortable in hospitals came to me naturally over time. Giving Reiki to clients during their surgeries has healed me of my squemishness and fears! On a recent case, I even strode across a blood-spattered floor without any hesitation in order to help my client. She was not responding to the doctors attempting to bring her out of anesthesia following her surgery. I walked to her side, with no reaction to the blood under my feet, so I could hold her hand and infuse her with Reiki while I called her name. She told me later that the Reiki and the sound of my voice calling to her were the things that drew her back into normal consciousness.

I'm now able to look directly at the operating table while people are experiencing surgery. Yet seeing sacred breast tissue in jars, knowing this is the stuff that has fed a woman's babies, or will never feed a living child, is enough to bring me to my knees. I understand with my whole heart and soul what these courageous women are giving up. I am humbled to be the one to pray for them and to bless that tissue as it leaves the OR for pathology, never to return. The courage these women demonstrate makes me brave enough to bear witness to their ordeals and to support their determination to live with joy.

Surgery is often followed by chemotherapy or radiation to hopefully ensure that the removed cancer does not reoccur. I support those in my care as they make their difficult decisions regarding whether and how to receive these extra treatments. Part of it is that surgery is very finite and direct; the results are pretty much understood before going in. The overall effects of chemotherapy and radiation are more nebulous. "You are more likely to be cancer-free five years from now if you do this" is what a patient will likely hear. Percentages given vary depending on the type of cancer, and sometimes the percentages are not that impressive, but medical studies do show that with extra treatment, the patient is more likely not only to survive but to remain cancer-free.

Reiki helps tremendously as one goes through this decision-making process by bringing clarity to the mind and emotions. It is also invaluable if it can be implemented whenever and wherever possible during the treatment process. Reiki brings balance to all the systems of the body and one major benefit is that it eases nausea while keeping side effects to a minimum. Additionally, the positive effect Reiki has on the mind and emotions cannot be overstated.

I quote Dr. Feldman's editorial in the medical journal *The Annals of Surgical Oncology*, where he describes the scientific research that supports his decision to include Reiki as part of a patient's breast cancer treatment:

> *At Columbia, we have initiated a study that incorporates the role of Reiki practitioners in applying mind–body principles and energy healing to help to prepare patients for breast cancer surgery and emotionally accept the loss of their breast(s). We must continue to strive to provide care that is patient-centered and reduces the stress and trauma of disease.*[15]

Dr. Feldman stands by his words. Not only do I work with him in the operating room, I also work with some of his patients who are receiving chemotherapy. On rare occasions, I've gone to Sloan-Kettering and Columbia Presbyterian hospitals to give Reiki during chemotherapy, but I don't prefer to do it that way. Although opinions differ, in a conversation with Luana DeAngelis, who is the founder and president of You Can Thrive, an organization that provides complementary services to women who are going through breast cancer, she told me, "My practitioners are not allowed to touch a client within forty-eight hours of their chemotherapy without wearing rubber gloves."

This conversation sent me on an investigative search, and I found a lot of information on this topic shared by cancer patients on the American Cancer Society blog in particular. Although there doesn't seem to be a definitive answer concerning the toxicity of chemotherapy to caregivers, I generally no longer give Reiki at the hospitals during chemotherapy, and following Ms. DeAngelis's lead, I also don't normally see patients right after they have had chemotherapy. In any case, my experience has proven that getting Reiki before chemotherapy is the best way to go. My clients who get Reiki before chemo have far fewer side effects and the chemotherapy generally seems to be more effective. In fact, in one case, a woman had Reiki before every one of her eight presurgery chemotherapy sessions. When she went for the surgery, the cancer was entirely gone!

Everyone who gets chemotherapy is well aware of the fact that they are being injected with poison to kill the cancer cells that might be lurking beneath the surface. It's unnerving to get a whiff of those infusions; you can smell the toxicity. All the time, I hear, "Raven, it goes so against my nature to take in such horrible substances. I feel like I'm doing the right thing in order to be cancer-free on the one hand, but I'm not feeling good about shooting up poison on the other." If a client is in my office having Reiki before chemotherapy, the client relaxes completely into a regular Reiki session. On those rare occasions when I've given Reiki at the hospital, I would not just give Reiki through the bottoms of the feet or through the top of the head, but I would also lead the client in visualizations.

"Close your eyes, and allow the Love that is Reiki to bring power and healing to the medicine coming into you. Relax and surrender into a place where all your cells are healing and performing perfectly as the powerful healing medicine, transformed by the love of Reiki, blesses you. Envision yourself as shining from the inside out—shining with health. Deepen this experience by surrounding yourself with golden light. Let the golden light intensify the power of the medicine and of your healing as you breathe in light ..." Visualization combined with Reiki makes the whole process so much easier! But in the hospital, the nurses are coming in and out, so it isn't the most relaxing experience.

In any case, not all doctors or hospitals allow Reiki practitioners to assist patients, and it's always definitely true that a Reiki practitioner would never be allowed to sit with a patient during radiation treatments. For anyone going through either or both of these kinds of treatments, I am offering up two meditations, one for chemotherapy and the other for radiation treatments. You can read them, or record yourself speaking the meditations and then listen to them through headphones before and after treatments. Ask your doctor if you can also listen during treatment. If the answer is yes, great; if the answer is no, then just continue to listen to the meditations at home. Try to do the meditations as often as you possibly can.

Guided Meditation: Chemotherapy

Close your eyes and begin to notice your breathing. Watch how the air is going in and out, across the tips of your nostrils. To still your mind, ask yourself, *I wonder what my next thought will be*, and allow your mind to ease itself into just watching the air passing through the very tips of your nostrils.

Thank the air you are breathing as it travels down your nasal passages, whether you see the experience, feel it, sense it, or just know that it's happening.

Begin to follow the air into your lungs, and go with it as it travels through your body. It might move quickly, or it might move slowly as it travels through you. There is no right or wrong, there's just the way it happens for you. Let yourself know how absolutely wonderful the air is; it blesses you continuously with life! Begin to thank the air from the center of your chest, from your heart. Emanate "thank you" into your body along your blood vessels, veins, and arteries; say "thank you" as the air passes through your heart.

As you thank the air, it begins to heal you very deeply. Your appreciation activates the healing properties inherent in the air itself. Notice how "thank you" begins to transform the air into a gentle, pulsing golden light, traveling through your bloodstream. Notice how the golden light is bringing feelings of love, safety, and comfort to your whole body. Rest in the beautiful energy of thanks.

Intensify your peace by calling to your Reiki master in spirit to infuse the golden light with even more healing. Rest.

Allow the love in the light to bring power and healing to the medicine coming into you. As the chemotherapy runs through you, the golden light automatically transforms it into deeply healing medicine. Surrender and allow healing to occur in every cell, just by resting and letting go.

Relax and surrender into a place where all your cells are healing and performing perfectly. Surrender to the healing that is naturally occurring within you as you rest in the love that is the light... Relax and surrender into a place where all your cells are healing and performing perfectly as the powerful healing medicine blesses you.

Envision yourself as shining with health from the inside out.

Deepen this experience of shining from the inside out by now surrounding yourself with golden light. Let the golden light intensify the power of the medicine and your healing as you breathe it in. You are healing as you think to yourself, *I am healthy, I am light, I am love, I am loved.* You can say these wonderful things to yourself as much as you like, for as long as you need.

Guided Meditation: Radiation

Close your eyes and begin to notice your breathing. Watch how the air is going in and out, across the tips of your nostrils. To still your mind, ask yourself, *I wonder what my next thought will be*, and allow your mind to ease itself into just watching the air passing through the very tips of your nostrils.

Thank the air you are breathing as it travels down your nasal passages, whether you see the experience, feel it, sense it, or just know that it's happening.

Say "thank you" to the air you are breathing and watch it go down your nasal passages, whether you see it, hear it, feel it, or just know that it's happening.

Begin to follow the air into your lungs, and go with it as it travels through your body. It might move quickly, or it might move slowly as it travels through you.

There is no right or wrong, there's just the way it happens for you. Let yourself know how absolutely wonderful the air is; it blesses you continuously with life! Begin to thank the air from the center of your chest, from your heart. Emanate "thank you" into your body along your blood vessels, veins, and arteries; say "thank you" as the air passes through your heart.

As you continue to thank the air, it begins to heal you even deeper. Your appreciation activates the healing properties inherent in the air itself. Notice how "thank you" begins to transform into a gentle, cooling sensation infused with healing traveling through your bloodstream. Notice how the cooling sensation is bringing feelings of love, safety, and comfort to your whole body.

Intensify your peace by calling to your Reiki master in spirit to infuse the cooling sensation with even more healing. Rest. Allow the love to bring soothing healing to the cooling sensation running through you.

The cooling continues to transform itself into ever-deepening healing medicine. Surrender and allow healing to occur in every cell, just by resting and letting go.

Relax and surrender into a place where all your cells are healing and performing perfectly. Surrender to the healing that is naturally occurring within you as you rest in the cooling love ... Relax and surrender into a place where all your cells are healing and performing perfectly as the healing sensation of coolness blesses you.

The cooling is soothing you—every cell, every part, every bit of you is soothed by the cooling that is running in your veins and arteries.

Call to your Reiki master in spirit and ask that the cooling sensation bring even more comfort to all parts of you: body, mind, emotions, and spirit. Rest in the comfort, cooling, and knowledge that you are healing right now. You are healing deeply within your cells. Rest in the healing; rest in the comfort that is love.

Allow the air around you to become very cool in temperature, and pretend that you are weightless. Float in the cool air. Ask your Reiki master in spirit to infuse the cool air around you with soothing healing properties. Now you breathe in the coolness and the healing. Allow it to travel into your lungs and through your body, filling your veins and arteries with health and comfort. Say thank you; float and breathe your way into dreaming. See, hear, sense, feel, or just know that you are floating in health and happiness, while saying to yourself, *I am healthy, I am strong, I am loved, I am love*. You can say these wonderful things to yourself as much as you would like, as much as you need to.

The amount of caring that these women put into us was… [overcome by emotion] now I know what angels look like.

—*Captain Jim Gormley,* FDNY[16]

CHAPTER 6

Reiki in Traumatic Events

I once read a story about a man who came upon a butterfly fighting to free itself from its cocoon. The man could see how the butterfly was struggling and he was worried, thinking something might be wrong. Wishing to make sure it would survive this terrible ordeal, he watched it closely. When the butterfly became exhausted, the man ran to get a pair of scissors. He cut the butterfly loose from its imprisoning cocoon, thinking he was saving it. But after that, the butterfly could never fly, because it needed that struggle to build strength in its wings.

This fable reminds me of myself, and the struggle I endured following 9/11 that made me strong to my core. Luckily, no one cut me out of my cocoon, so in all of its intensity, the aftermath of September 11th became the smithy that wrought my life as a Reiki master into one as strong as steel. Even though the time period was short in duration compared to all the years of my life, those eight and a half months of volunteering affected me more than any other time before or since, more than I could have ever imagined it would. I was forced to learn what it meant to be brave and I learned how important it is to take care of myself as I do my work. And I came to realize, more than ever before, the undeniable and powerful way in which Reiki can bring help to those in need.

Traumatic events provide opportunities to face fears, to look fears in the face, and to grow wings from the strength you develop through overcoming them. This kind of growth comes when bringing gifts of healing to any traumatic event, including those caused by natural disasters. I have colleagues who traveled to New Orleans after Hurricane Katrina and to Haiti after the earthquake in order to bring relief, comfort, and healing to the people affected by those terrible events. The strengths my colleagues developed from their experiences are undeniable. As for me, I got my wings in the aftermath of the tragedy that took place right here in New York City.

In the days right after 9/11, Equinox Fitness opened the doors of all their clubs throughout New York City to the rescue and recovery workers who might want some rest, relaxation, or even a workout, if that's what they needed to deal with their emotional pain. For the first time in my life, my meditation classes were filled with not just the usual Equinox members, but with members of the NYPD and FDNY. In each class, I prayed to the Reiki masters in spirit, asking them to help all those present with their terrible emotional wounds. At the end of each class, I would stand in silence with my hands held up, sending Reiki out with the prayer that it would assist anyone in the room whose spirit gave permission for them to receive the healing.

It was after one of those meditation classes that a police sergeant came up to me and said, "I was on duty that day and I sent in some of those guys who died. I don't want to go down to the Trade Center ever again, but I have no choice, and you know, there are ghosts walking around on that pile. I don't know how to handle that." I know he wanted me to help him with this, but I was so shocked I didn't know what to say.

Within the first few weeks, John and I went with a Reiki table to my local firehouse on Amsterdam Avenue and 66th Street. Their loss was terrible; except for one man, they lost every single person who was on duty that fateful morning. Because John looks so much like his Irish dad, in a city where firefighting runs in many Irish families, John was easily accepted. The firefighters were able to receive Reiki from him, while giving him T-Shirts and invitations to return to provide more Reiki.

Meanwhile, my husband Michael was desperately trying to help our friend, Zack, who was searching for his sister. Zack's sister, Elizabeth, was an attorney for one of the big firms on an upper floor in the South Tower, and the last anyone knew, from a call she had made to her husband, she was on her way out of the building. While Zack was in the throes of endless trips back and forth between the hospitals all over the city and the temporary Family Assistance Center set up in the armory on Lexington Avenue, my husband was making phone calls and searching the Internet for clues as to Elizabeth's whereabouts. Elizabeth's name appeared on a list of survivors, but there the trail ended. Rumors were flying of victims who couldn't remember who they were who had been taken to hospitals in other states. Michael was tracking down every lead he could find, calling hospitals as far away as Kentucky.

After a few weeks had gone by, a friend of mine who was a yoga teacher called to see if Michael and I would accompany her down to what was now being called "Ground Zero." I wanted to send Reiki directly into the rubble, so we decided to go. My heart held onto a slim hope that even now, almost three weeks later, it might help Elizabeth, who was still missing, and any people still buried.

We made our way downtown and met crowds as we came up from the subway station. People were hysterical, crying all around us, and there were places set up where people could pray with ministers and priests. It was a struggle to get through the crowds of people, as well as the barricades set up all along the streets to control the crowds.

When we rounded one corner, I couldn't go any farther. What was before my eyes was too much for me to bear: piles of debris, stories tall, and the standing remains of the steel tridents that were destined to become famous as a symbol of 9/11. What brought me to my knees was the sight of all the windows in the surrounding buildings that had been blown out. They looked like eyes that had been violently poked out in the throes of torture. I wept uncontrollably, feeling the utter and complete destruction and despair sweeping across the area.

I held up my palms and sent Reiki to all the people both above and below the rubble whose spirits might wish to receive it, while I silently prayed for Elizabeth to be found. I have no idea how long we were there. It was surreal and timeless. After a while, Michael, with his sensitive lungs, started to cough from all the smoke and fumes, so we had to go.

Elizabeth's body was found in the rubble within twelve hours of our being there. It was a very different kind of Reiki blessing than what any of us would have ever wanted, but it was a blessing nevertheless. As things would turn out, many people were never found at all.

I heard of a wellness center called Olive Leaf that was sending healers of all sorts to crucial locations around the city. After a thorough interview and confirmation of my Reiki-master status, I was issued papers granting me access to the NYC Family Assistance Center (FAC) and the Office of Chief Medical Examiner (OCME) where they wanted me to offer Reiki. There I would find massage therapists, Reiki masters, craniosacral therapists, reflexologists, chiropractors, and acupuncturists. From everywhere in the country, people hitchhiked or left jobs, clients, children, and families to be in New York. It was a group of volunteers with skills that had never before been allowed on the scene of *any* disaster, and yet there were hundreds of us.

The FAC was an immense labyrinth of aisles and desks. It was set up with places to sit, cry, or fall asleep. We were dealing with unprecedented disaster, and the FAC existed solely to serve the family members of the victims, helping them with more things than you can imagine. There was paperwork to fill out. They needed lawyers. They needed counseling. They needed someone to remind them to sit down. They needed someone to remind them to eat. They needed everything. There were volunteers of every profession offering aid to these poor people for free.

Someone had lovingly set up our treatment area. Eight massage tables were separated from our "waiting room" by thin white sheets hanging from poles. Setting down my things next to one of the tables, I peered out from between the sheets into the waiting room area filled with people who looked like the walking dead. Their eyes were almost indistinguishable within their grief-swollen faces.

The site coordinator brought a petite Latino woman with salt-and-pepper hair into my cloth office. She stood before me with blank eyes.

"Please make yourself comfortable on the table, okay?" I said to her as I helped her up and she lay down.

She was silent, compliant, and unresponsive. I positioned my hands and received my green light to begin the Reiki. In the first instant, I knew something was very, very wrong. I could see her body before me, but under my hands I felt nothing—no spirit, no life force, no energy at all. It felt like she was missing from inside her own body. I eventually came to realize what I had read about years before in Sandra Ingerman's book, *Soul Retrieval: Mending the Fragmented Self*: this woman's emotional pain was so great that her spirit had "left" in order for her to survive this ordeal.[17] She was a human shell, breathing. Having never been in a situation like this before, I didn't know what to do, so I just followed through with what I knew: I sent Reiki into her body. As I got closer to the twenty-minute mark that would end her session, I began to feel a profound and loving spirit next to me, and I heard myself saying out loud, "Michael, Gabriel, Jesus." The woman started to cry and told me that her husband was named Michael. He had been in Windows on the World, the famous restaurant at the top of the North Tower. She and her family were still holding out hope that he was alive, but he was gone. He had just come to tell her that he was with Jesus and the angels. When she was able to get up, I helped her down and walked her back to the waiting arms of her daughter.

The level of love I felt for the people who came to be on my table was something indescribable, and I wasn't the only one to experience it. All of the practitioners felt like we were administering powerful, unexpected transmissions from a divine source so present it was almost visible to the naked eye. And this included the psychotherapists and mental-health workers who had arrived from across the country to lend their assistance. We worked in tandem.

On my next daytime shift at the FAC, police were bringing family members to our tables directly from Ground Zero. There was a woman brought to my table by a bilingual site coordinator, because the woman spoke no English. As she lay down on the table, she looked out at me with vacant eyes. It was the site coordinator who told her in Spanish to close them. I began the session, and it wasn't a surprise to discover that, once again, I couldn't feel anyone inside the body under my hands. It wasn't until the twenty minutes were up and I began to whisper, "I ask that this Reiki energy heal, harmonize, and balance…"Apparently she heard me and snapped back in. She started to cry so piteously with wrenching sobs, trying to tell me things in Spanish, which I didn't understand. The site coordinator heard the woman crying and ran in to help, beginning to translate, "My son, my son, my beautiful son! He worked in the restaurant on the top of the building. He came here from our home in Peru. We are very poor. He came to make money for our family. He died on his birthday, he died on his birthday…" I held her and cried right along with her.

I was called to assist one of the other therapists who did reflexology. There was a woman on his table who couldn't be touched. She didn't speak English, and no one could figure out what language she spoke. She was crying, and she just winced whenever he touched her, so he asked if I could please do touchless Reiki for her. I felt so bad for her; it had to be terrible to be isolated within herself, as we couldn't understand her.

"Telling" was part of what everyone who came to us had to do sooner or later. If they couldn't speak in the beginning, they would be telling us things by the end. Everyone had to tell their personal stories of where they were when the planes hit and how this was affecting them personally. It was never-ending, and it was really difficult to constantly bear witness. Reiki itself is always and forever only positive. Even though I kept myself in an energetically protected state while I worked, by surrounding myself in white light and staying in constant contact with Gabriel, my human heart was very disturbed by seeing the emotional toll that this event had created. It felt as though the whole human population of the earth was in pain. In the case of this particular woman, she was eased by the Reiki and fell asleep on the table. At the end of our time together, she hugged me before she went away. I later got a note from her on a pink Post-it written in choppy English, thanking me for making her feel loved. It is still one of my most prized possessions.

Over the next several weeks, I treated mother after mother, widow after widow, all with their empty bodies and the haunting desperation in their eyes. I saw their faces in my sleep. There were nights when I'd come home from my shift and just sob. On those nights, Michael would rock me, try to comfort me, and my dog, Echo, would kiss me endlessly to try to make me feel better.

In all the activity, it never occurred to me to take time for myself, though in hindsight I realize I wasn't taking the best care of myself. During every single shift, I knew I was representing all the other Reiki practitioners in the world who might wish they could be the ones providing the comfort and healing. I knew I was lucky to be there. I considered it a sacred honor to be bringing Reiki to this situation, and I would never let anyone down by backing out.

Instead of quitting, I did my shifts, repeating to myself, *I ask to be the hollow bone, I ask to be the hollow bone*, a catchphrase taught to me by a shaman to help me do what Reiki masters are meant to do. In the face of the overwhelming trauma, that phrase worked like a charm. Just by saying it to myself, I would be able to empty myself to let the Reiki flow in and through, no matter what was going on around me. Yet the wife, mother, and woman in me couldn't help but feel the unrelenting suffering experienced by the people beneath my hands. I went in there every shift and felt like I'd lost my own son or my own husband, day after day after day.

The last woman I treated at the FAC had come from India in hopes of finding her child. Like so many others before her, as she lay down on my table, she looked at me with vacant eyes, like she was an empty shell—she was just a void carved out by pain. As I began the Reiki session, her spirit suddenly returned. This poor, brokenhearted mother reared up, grabbed my shirt, and yanked me right down to her face. With a wild look in her eyes, she began to cry out, "Tell me! Tell me! Can you see my daughter?" And then she was screaming, beating on her chest with her fists, repeating in shrieks, "Every morning I light the candles, every morning I light all of the candles in the house. Every morning I light all the candles, so my daughter can see in the dark." I never saw such grief; it took three mental-health volunteers to calm her down. This is the kind of pain that can make you lose your mind. And to be honest, it scared the hell out of me.

When volunteers ran into each other on the street, we'd talk about our assigned locations.

"I can't take it at the medical examiners', so I'm doing my shifts at the Family Center," most would say.

But I had begun to feel just the opposite. Give me the cops and the firemen who were supposedly "used" to such things. Let me do sessions on the DMORTs (Disaster Mortuary Operational Response Teams) who'd arrived from all over the country, trained to handle disasters. They could bear it all, couldn't they?

Never mind that they smelled of the smoke from the burning bodies, rubber, jet fuel, and steel we were always trying to forget—the scent that permeated every cell of our city all the way from the World Trade Center site up to the Bronx, out to Queens, Brooklyn, and even New Jersey. Never mind that they were straight off the pile, doing work of some mysterious nature as they waded through all that death.

I couldn't quit. I had to do what I could to help. I knew so many needed the powerful love that Reiki brings. So I requested a transfer to the OCME, the morgue.

Little did I know, each step I was taking was only bringing me closer to the pit.

The next week, I flashed my identification badge at a police barricade and was escorted to the OCME. Our designated area was at the back of the church tent, where services were held twenty-four hours a day, seven days a week. Ministers, priests, rabbis, you name it, they were there reciting prayers. We could hear their soothing murmuring from the tables we had lined up on the other side of a wall of sheets.

From 30th Street to First Avenue and all the way to the East Side Highway was disaster central for the City of New York. Police, fire marshals, DMORT, FDNY, Navy, Army, FBI, medical examiners—this was the bustling and overstressed population to whom I'd now be administering my services. Police officers from every branch of law enforcement, state troopers, corrections officers from prisons like Riker's Island, police from towns throughout the state of New York, all were taking shifts to help out. This was the crew handling the crime scene, bringing in the dead from Ground Zero and identifying the deceased. Most of them had never even experienced a massage before, let alone been exposed to most of the alternative therapies we had up for offer.

Site coordinators did their best to inform the depleted men and women of the unfamiliar names of therapies—Reiki, acupuncture, craniosacral, etc.—as they gently guided them to our tables until we were full to capacity. I worked on Frank, a towering NYPD officer who went into a bliss state; I could see goose bumps moving down his arms while the Reiki poured into his tired body. After, he said, "Lady! That was awesome! How do you say the name of what that is again?"

Then came a chaplain from Kenya. He was followed by a cop from Suffolk County who refused to take off his holster, so I did Reiki on a fully armed man for the first (but not the last) time in my life. As I was to discover, everyone was obsessed with knowing the whereabouts of their gun at all times: no one was convinced the disaster was really over. In their minds, they had to be ready to protect themselves and the rest of us in an instant.

A firefighter lay down, explaining that due to the appalling number of FDNY lost in the collapse, he'd been promoted to fire marshal. Now it was his job to identify the bodies of fallen firefighters. He fell asleep on the table in ten seconds. A moment later, the spirit of one of his friends who'd died came to stand next to me. Together we watched a tear roll down the new fire marshal's cheek as he dreamed.

Next came a forensic dentist. I touched his shoulders lightly at the start of the session, and I gasped while my head flooded with images. I was seeing what he'd seen: pieces of human bodies, scraps of hair, and dried blood. I shook my head, all the while channeling the love that is Reiki through my body. Then there was the female sergeant who lay down so calmly on my table before shoving her fist in her mouth to stifle the sobs she couldn't afford her men to hear.

That first day, not caring who saw me, I cried all the way home on the bus.

Around the end of October, I'd just arrived at the OCME carrying a much-needed cup of coffee that I got from the Salvation Army food truck. As I walked through the cloth doorway, one of the directors from Olive Leaf was giving a small lecture to the therapists who'd assembled. "Geranium oil takes away bad memories," she said as she passed the brown glass bottle around so we could all savor the scent. "Isn't it nice? Make sure to ask them if it's okay to put a dab under their nostrils before you begin their treatments." She didn't dare say what kinds of smells it also helped to cover up.

What bizarre alternate reality had I landed in? One where we were asking police officers if we could anoint them with oils so they could bear what they now had to do every day? They walked over the rubble, every one of them suffering from exhaustion, even as they brought us candy, hats, and memorial ribbons, little gestures of their gratitude to us for helping them.

It was at times like this when I recognized the extreme turn my life had taken, that I would just step outside my body and watch what I was doing, like an observer. That was how I handled it for myself. But even though I felt like Alice falling down the rabbit hole sometimes, there was no time to stay focused on me or how extremely my life as a practitioner had changed. Healing work needed to be done!

My first real DMORT friend was Alan Clark from Beaver, Oklahoma. A funeral director and a DMORT team leader, Alan was a devoted family man, which made him extra compassionate. He was also very accustomed to being kind to people who are grieving.

"Howdy there, I'm Alan. What's your name, little lady?" With that Southern accent and warm smile, I took no offense—I could only smile back.

"I'm Raven."

"Well, Miss Raven, they tell me you do somethin' I never heard of. But you look like a nice person, so I figure it ought to be good."

With that he lay down on the table, and right away, I could feel him slip into the deep inner calm that Reiki brings, followed by an emotional release. He started to cry. He started thinking about things that I could see inside my head—buildings destroyed, kids on a swing set, the mess under his feet at Ground Zero.

When the session was over, Alan thanked me from the bottom of his heart.

"Miss Raven, I was at Oklahoma City after the bombing, where we laid so many little children to rest, and when I was leaving to come here, I saw some kids on a set of swings, and I thought of all those little ones who died in Oklahoma, knowing I was about to see even worse things here. Thanks for this. What you're doing really helps." He left the tent, but he came back a little while later with a plastic cup full of Hershey's Kisses for me.

"Thanks again!" he said with a smile.

Alan came to try Reiki again a few days later. After his second session was over, he sat up and said to me, "Miss Raven, there's only one massage therapist in my little town, but I'm gonna tell her she's just GOT to learn Reiki!" Needless to say, Alan became one of my regulars. We became great friends.

Here in New York City, being a cop or a firefighter can run in the family. In many cases, the people we worked on lost not just a friend, but in some cases, even a family member. By now, we were beginning to witness survivor guilt, which was making it even harder for those who desperately needed our services to take advantage of them.

I was a few hours past the geranium oil conversation when I first met Seamus Ward. Seamus was an FDNY fire marshal who came to the OCME to identify the body of a firefighter; while he was there, he was encouraged by the OCME site coordinator, Linda Hazlett, to try Reiki. Site coordinators functioned like angels of mercy, convincing these needy public servants to take advantage of what we were offering. "If you can't do it for yourself, do it for your family," Linda would say. Or if that didn't work, "You have to take care of yourself. If you can't do it for you, then do it for me, and for all the other citizens of New York who are depending on you." Linda was very skilled at convincing.

Once there, it fell to us therapists to be sensitive to the needs of whomever happened to be on our table so they remained long enough to receive the gifts of our services. Oftentimes, their nerves were overwrought and they were jumpy, not to mention they considered themselves to be exhibiting extreme weakness just by being on a table in the first place.

Seamus was Irish through and through, with red hair, blue eyes, and an Irish Catholic mother who was grateful to Jesus for keeping both her FDNY sons alive on September 11th. He sat very still as we spoke softly together.

"What is *ray-kay*?" he asked me with his thick Brooklyn accent.

"Well, it's a gentle form of hands-on healing."

"Is it religious? Because after all this, I don't believe in God anymore. Do I have to believe something?"

"Great question. No, you don't have to believe a thing. You just lie down and relax. I do the rest. Don't you think you could use a little rest right now?"

"Well, I guess so. I've been up for about two days straight. But I have to put my gun under the pillow. I'm not letting you take my gun." By this time I knew fire marshals in New York City were part of law enforcement, so they carry guns; his requirement was not unfamiliar to me.

"Okay, Seamus, put your gun under the pillow then. You're right, it'll be safe there." He took the clip of bullets out, put the clip in his pocket and the gun under the pillow, satisfying his need to know the exact location of his firearm.

With his gun secured to his liking, Seamus lay himself down on the table. I covered him up with a white sheet and put a folded-up pillowcase over his eyes to block out the light. He was asleep before I could count to five. Seamus slept soundly through his session, in spite of the fact that people were running past the tent with their radios blaring ominous reports of the things that were happening down at Ground Zero. I closed my eyes and felt Reiki rush through me down to the soul-drenching extent to which Seamus needed it. Reiki was pouring into not just his cells, but into his very life itself.

For me, all the conversations in the tent began to blend together. Words from prayers in the church part of the tent were mixing with those of another fire marshal on the next table. He was telling his therapist the harrowing tale of having to fill out paperwork four times for the same firefighter for reasons I don't care to repeat. I was quickly sinking deeper into the Reiki zone, while that fire marshal's words mixed together with those of an NYPD on another table, who was telling *his* therapist about the pain of finding his best friend buried in the rubble. I began to pray, "Please help me to be strong. These people need us, and they need Reiki so badly!"

When the session was over, I let Seamus have a few more moments of uninterrupted sleep before I gently shook him awake. As he slowly opened his eyes, they were shining with wonder. I knew he was glad that he had come. Sitting up and reaching for his gun, I could tell he felt a bit shy about getting it out from under the pillow after I had just given him something that was so obviously from the land of peace. In my wish to soothe him, I calmly asked, "Oh, is that a Beretta?" (It was the only gun name I could remember from watching TV.)

"No, it's a Smith and Wesson."

"Oh. Does it fire shots one after the other?"

"Yes," he told me. He began to explain everything about it, showing me the safety catch and how the clip of bullets slipped into the handle. As he was carefully showing me all this, I got the feeling that underneath it all, he just didn't want to leave the tent and jump back into all the drama that life had become.

"Would you like to hold it?" I could tell by his face that he was shocked at himself, and sorry he had asked me such a question. It was unheard of for a civilian to be offered a gun, but I understood that he felt a kinship with me that had been forged by the Reiki. I couldn't bear the look in his eyes of such regret. It was a very complicated moment in which it was imperative to me that he left his session feeling not embarrassed and distressed but comforted and healed.

As I pondered what to do, my heart told me that his spirit felt I represented a bridge to sanity. So I said, "Yes." He removed the clip of bullets and handed it to me. I actually held a gun, because I knew in the depths of my soul that this man needed me to do so. And maybe he even thought that some of that "ray-kay" would get into his firearm, as it had gotten into him.

It was only after Seamus had left that I remembered I was supposed to ask him if he wanted to smell geranium oil…

For all those who came in and knew about our services, there were many who still had no idea that we were there. Some of those who crossed our paths eyed us—alternative care workers—with suspicion or ignored us altogether. But from day one, the DMORT squad members were totally open, and even thrilled, that we were there. Maybe it was because, based on past experiences, they were most aware of what trauma is and how to avoid it. Our country has these DMORT people, experts in all areas of forensics, whom they call upon to help with handling remains and identifying victims who have died whenever there is a disaster. The squads start out as volunteers, but if the crisis is severe enough and they are needed for an extended period of time, then the government pays them to stay to do their work.

I became friends with a woman named Gayle Onnen of the DMORT squad. Gayle came for Reiki whenever she could. She cried softly while I gave her Reiki, and just as I was completing our second session together, I heard the loud rumbling of a fleet of motorcycle engines, signaling that a police escort was accompanying the body of a firefighter or police officer being brought to the morgue from Ground Zero. This was the first time I had to follow the Olive Leaf instructions given to us for this scenario.

Gayle and I, along with everyone else inside the tent, went outside to stand side by side with all the officers lining the street. Five men had been found together; they were being brought in five different ambulances. As the ambulances turned down 30th Street and slowly made their way to the back entry to the morgue, the call to salute was given by a commanding officer. We all stood with our hands raised to our brows in salute to the fallen heroes. It was absolutely surreal and it struck me like a ton of bricks just how vastly my life had changed from the one I once knew. My heart swelled up with hurt and something burst inside me. I felt sobs starting to shake through my chest. *I serve life and healing!* I thought, *How can I be standing here like this?* I tried to turn my face so they couldn't see me cry. I felt like I was letting my country down by crying, because with so much anguish everywhere, and so much at stake, crying in front of each other seemed like too much of a luxury. Panic rose inside me. I thought, *Oh, no! What if my tears cause others to start breaking down?* Trying to get a grip, I commanded myself, *NO! STOP! We owe it to each other to stand strong so we can all continue!* Still, it was of no use. In spite of anything I might *tell* myself, tears were already streaming down my face, and just as I feared, all the police officers and medical examiners nearby turned and stared. I wiped my face on my sleeve, fixing my eyes on the vehicles. When the bodies had all been delivered into the morgue, the call to stop saluting was made. I turned, retreating into the tent.

Midway through a nose blow, a shuffling of feet made me turn in surprise to find a line of burly guys forming, all waiting for me to work on them. I believe my tears helped them understand I wouldn't judge their vulnerability and they could be whatever they needed to be in my presence. That day, as police officers and FDNY climbed up onto my table, they told me about their wives and children, their hopes for the future, who they knew who died. When I apologized to the last police officer in line, telling him I'd run out of time for the day and had a meditation class to teach, he offered to drive me to Equinox on Broadway and 19th Street so I could give him just a few minutes on my table. It was the first time in my life I'd ever been inside a police car.

I want to state unequivocally that Reiki is always safe, always helpful, and can only heal. When a practitioner gives Reiki, we open ourselves up to receive and then give that healing power to our clients; we do not absorb anything from the person we are working on. We know how to protect ourselves energetically; it's part of our training. Yet, I didn't know how to protect myself emotionally from the overwhelming feelings of grief that everyone around me was feeling.

I've always been sensitive, and as I entered this situation with the pure desire to bring relief to those in need, I hadn't been told how to separate myself from the human feelings of those around me who were in the throes of such extreme emotional pain. I didn't know how to take care of myself in this situation. Yes, I knew how to energetically protect myself while doing my work, and my energy meditation teacher, Lille O'Brien, had taught me how to spin energy out of me that might have strayed in. In this case, however, my human heart was breaking. And although all of us practitioners were definitely in a situation where we needed to be taking care of ourselves, thoughts of self-care didn't even come to mind when faced with the emotional trauma that everyone working on the pile was undergoing. I just carried on day after day, hanging up the holsters and bulletproof vests of those who came to my table so these exhausted men and women could rest while I provided them with the healing energy they needed. All these people were desperate for the Reiki help.

January 2002 came, and the space we were occupying at the OCME was needed for more refrigeration trucks where the remains of the Ground Zero victims were being held for identification. When Linda Hazlett told one of the lieutenants of the Port Authority Police Department (PAPD) that we had to leave the OCME, he asked if we'd consider relocating to the PAPD trailer at Ground Zero.

Responsible for the policing and protection of all the bridges, tunnels, and airports in the New York and New Jersey area, the PAPD were also responsible for the World Trade Center site as well. Their headquarters had been in the North Tower. They lost thirty-seven officers when the towers fell, the largest number of police officers ever lost in one incident in the history of our country. Though their department is responsible for so much, their force is comparatively small. Virtually every man or woman we'd meet had a friend or relative who'd been lost.

Because their duties in the rest of the city were now split among such a small number of surviving officers, the decision was made to assign only certain officers to be at Ground Zero. This meant that whoever was stationed at the pile would be there for the duration of the excavation efforts. The strain on everyone was unimaginable. Unlike the NYPD or FDNY, who were rotated in and out, these PAPD officers stayed from day one until the very end of the cleanup. Retired PAPD officers called "Team Romeo" had come forward to help out.

It was a surprisingly mild January night as I approached the checkpoint for the PAPD trailer on the northwest perimeter of Ground Zero. My knees felt weak. The OCME had been all the way up on 30th Street; I had never stood on Ground Zero itself. A sergeant was assigned to give me a tour of the "station," which was actually a jumble of trailers, similar to what you'd see on a construction site. The trailers were a configuration of one large main room, a separate locker room for the guys, another "office" for the commanding officers, and another smaller room officially designated for the sergeants of the PAPD where we were assigned. Linda had made arrangements with a few of the guys from Corrections (prison guards) to deliver our things the day before from the OCME.

I soon found out that nobody had any idea that I was coming.

Conversation stopped midsentence as people turned to look me over. The sergeant who had given the tour left me standing in the middle of the main room and took off to go down to the pit. I felt like I'd walked into a small-town diner. Being such a small community, friends and relatives of the PAPD officers milled about and stared with open curiosity. Was I somebody's wife? A sister perhaps? But no one spoke to me; they just watched me as I made my way back to the room where our belongings had been set up earlier: two massage tables, two massage chairs, a portable CD player, some candles, and even some aromatherapy items (including my new bottle of geranium oil).

I closed the door and took refuge on a plastic chair. The energy in the place was so chocked up with testosterone I could almost taste it. These men were tough and I was on their turf. *What on earth are these men going to make of me?* I thought. As I gathered up my nerve, going back out into the big room full of officers, I really had no idea how to begin with them.

Ever-present in the main room was the blackboard that carried the names of the thirty-seven missing PAPD officers on it; along with the officers, the PAPD had lost Sirius, their beloved K-9 yellow Labrador who'd been killed in the collapse of the North Tower. It was January and there weren't many names with stars next to them (a star next to a name meant that either a body or some piece or identifiable remains had been found). The rest were just missing.

Standing in front of the blackboard was a towering freight train of a man. He was rubbing his tired eyes with two balled fists, making him look for a moment, despite his size, like a lost and bewildered little boy. I gathered up my courage and walked over to him.

"Hey," I said tentatively, "My name's Raven." He turned to look at me, and I could see a spark of humor in his eyes as he inclined his head, waiting for me to continue.

"Um, we've come down here to try and help you guys feel better. You might not have ever heard of what I do, but I've worked on the New York Giants. Do you know about Charles Way? Well, I did Reiki on his knee, and it got better."

He sized me up with a smirk. "*Reiki*? Ha! I *rakey-rakey* all day in the pit," he chuckled. It was contagious.

"Very funny." I broke into a smile. "I'm just saying... if it worked on a professional football player..."

"Well," he said, looking around. "To tell you the truth, my knee is bothering me, too. I fell off a roof." I waited as he considered. "I guess it couldn't hurt to give it a try."

Smiling under the flourescent lights, I guided him back to the sergeants' office that was now a treatment room, lit a few candles, closed the door, and clicked on the music while he reclined on the table.

"Just relax," I said as I put a lavender-scented eye pillow over his eyes. As I closed my eyes and began the session, the powerful presence of a man came to stand beside me. I could see him clearly in my mind; he was tall and robustly built with peppered hair and mischievous blue eyes. Clearly he'd died in the tower collapse.

I have something you gotta tell him, he communicated, gesturing to my hulking client lying on the table.

My mouth went dry. Wonderful. *My first day in the police trailer and now I'm supposed to be giving this man, who barely wants to be here anyway, a message from the beyond?* I thought. I transmitted back to the spirit, *I'm very sorry, but I just can't do that. I don't know this man at all, and I don't want to upset him!*

Don't worry, the spirit assured me, *He wants to hear what I have to say. It's important to him.*

Okay, okay, I sighed.

"Sir," I began, "I don't know exactly how to tell you this, but . . . there's a spirit here, and he wants to tell you something."

"What? Holy Jesus, what is it?" He started to sit up, causing the eye pillow to fall off. He saw the look of panic on my face and laid back down, grabbing the eye pillow and putting it back over his eyes. "It's okay, miss, just tell me."

I positioned my hands over the man's heart and paused a moment, trying to tune in better, then opened my mind to receive the message, which I spoke into the room.

"Well," I said, "he's a middle-aged man, I can see him clear as day, and he's saying, 'Sticks and stones can break my bones. But I'm not blood and bone. There is no death. There's only life.'"

The man's breath caught in his throat. A single tear rolled out from under the eye pillow toward his ear as he lay on the table. He pursed his lips to control the emotion. When he could talk, he said, "We used to say that rhyme to each other as kids. That's my brother."

I felt a shock of heartbreak ratcheting through him and tried to send as much Reiki into his heart center as I could.

"He was in the tower," he continued before his voice broke. "We haven't found him yet. I guess we won't be finding his body, but at least now I know he's okay."

At that moment, the door, which was closed, burst open and a commanding officer stood there, his jaw tensed up so tightly I could see the veins in his neck. I nearly jumped out of my skin. "What the hell is going on in here?" he boomed. "Who's in charge?"

I thought he must be talking to the guy on the table who didn't move a muscle. The commander glared at me and yelled, "Are *you* in charge?"

The past few months flashed by in my head. I never felt less in charge of anything in all my life. The ridiculousness of his question caused a laugh to escape from deep inside me.

"*Maybe*..." was all I could manage in the face of his fury.

"Get into my office!"

Oh no... this was not the way I wanted to begin my first shift in the PAPD trailer. I followed him into the commanding officers' room as he slammed the door closed behind me and started to shout.

"What in the *hell* do you think you're doing? Do you know where you are? What the hell..."

My eyes started filling up with tears as I fixed my gaze on something, anything... his nametag. *Lieutenant Doubraski.*

"Lieutenant, you're yelling at me!" My voice was shaking. "We're only here to help you guys. We're just volunteer therapists who were asked to come here. We're just trying to help!"

I could see him start to panic. He was a gentleman, a public servant. And I was a woman, crying in his office.

"Oh, look, miss, please don't cry. Okay, you can do it." He let out a sigh. "We just can't have even a whiff of impropriety here. The press is in and out of here constantly. The whole world is watching us. You can do whatever it is you do, okay, but keep the lights on, the door open, and no more of that music."

Relieved, I nodded. It's funny now to think that Lieutenant Doubraski would go on to become one of my biggest supporters and closest friends.

That night when my shift was over, I took the subway home. I was mulling over all that happened during my first hours at Ground Zero, and was thinking of the spirit who had come to let his brother know he was safely on the other side. That's when the subway stopped at 42nd Street, where I was changing trains. Just as I stepped out onto the platform, still thinking of the deceased officer, there was a loud shout ricocheting through the station that sounded like the call to salute I had heard so many times at the OCME. Without thinking, I stopped dead in my tracks and raised my hand to my brow. In that very moment, I heard the mournful sounds of "Amazing Grace" being played on bagpipes. The haunting melody, played by a street musician, filled the whole subway station as I stood with my hand raised in salute. I felt in my heart that the brother who had died had somehow orchestrated these events so I would know he was now going home into the light. Sure enough, as the music was playing, I heard a voice whisper in my head, *Thank you*, and my heart was touched with love. I knew the power of Reiki had bestowed yet another blessing.

Despite the treatment I'd done with the "gentle giant" of a brother, as I'd come to think of him, the men were still extremely shy and avoided me and the other volunteers. So I decided to hit up Lieutenant William Doubraski.

"Hey, Lieutenant."

"Yes, Ms. Keyes?" He looked nervous already.

"Uh … would you like to try a little Reiki?" He looked at me in horror.

"No, ma'am, I cannot do that."

"But Lieutenant," I pleaded, "Your guys aren't coming in. It's obvious they think we're some sort of 'woo-woo' freaks. Maybe if you just came in …"

"Listen, Ms. Keyes. I have to lead these guys. This isn't playtime here. I mean, for Christ's sake, I'm a former Marine!"

I looked him squarely in the eyes. "Lieutenant, you know what your guys are going through down there in the pit, and I know you want them to be okay. You want them to take care of themselves and to come out of all this somehow whole. They won't be able to accept *any* of the help we've come here to bring unless you go first. You have to lead them into what's good for their own health."

He looked at me a long moment, then dropped his head, considering while he looked at his shoes.

"All right. Fine." With that he marched into our treatment room and got up on the table. Of course, he fell asleep almost instantly.

When the session was over, Lieutenant Doubraski was energized and almost glowing. He beamed at me. I watched as he walked into the big room, trying to phrase his advice correctly, and cleared his throat, trying to sound casual. "Hey, guys, I just got some of that Reiki, and it's really good. I want you all to try it! It's really good for you." And so they did.

A man named Keith became one of my regulars after his first trial of Reiki. He loved it and came in for mini-sessions whenever he had a minute. His back was bothering him, he was getting migraine headaches, and his chest hurt. Reiki soothed him. I sensed a lot of damage inside the chests of most of the people who'd breathed the air at the site while everything was still burning.

Then there was Jimmy O'Hanlon with the grin that could light up the room. All the papers for his retirement had burned up in the collapse of the North Tower, but he worked alongside the retired officers known as Team Romeo just the same. They were a unit that was revered for coming to the aid of the PAPD as volunteers without pay at a time when their experience was needed. I can still see Jimmy now in my mind's eye in those brown overalls they all wore, holding his hardhat in his hand, with sparkling green eyes and smiling at me. From Reiki to massage to aromatherapy, I couldn't name Jimmy's favorite healing technique because he loved them all. A natural leader, it was because of Jimmy that other workers were able to come onto our tables for some relief.

And there was Henry LaLlave, known to everyone as Hank, who was an angel in uniform. He came nearly every day for Reiki, and we became really good friends. He'd been in the war in Viet Nam, and had witnessed the 1993 bombing of the World Trade Center. He was weary and beaten down from seeing so much death in his life. Hank had been stationed at the World Trade Center for eighteen years, where he'd patrolled the buildings on the night shift. He loved the buildings with such passion I wondered if he were an architect instead of a man of the law. Sadly for Hank, he knew not only police officers who'd died that day, but dozens of men and women who worked in the buildings. His bravery, mixed with pain, were things I kept close to my heart as we continued, through Reiki, to develop our friendship over the months to come.

As time went by, we had fewer volunteers showing up. People were either burned out or had to return home. But for those of us who remained, we mixed and matched our various healing techniques, matching our clients' needs to our skills, as they marched in and out of the pit, coming and going in shifts.

I arrived for my Thursday afternoon shift on March 7, 2002, not realizing that the healing services had officially been cancelled for the day. The site had been shut down to accommodate a tour of Ground Zero for pilots from American and United Airlines. I had my cell phone up to my ear, listening to the cancellation message just as I was arriving at the check-in point. I saw Lieutenant Doubraski getting out of his squad car on the other side of the barricade. I snapped my cell phone closed as he ran up to me, reaching out to take my arm. "Raven, thank God you're here! The guys really need you today!" No further explanation was forthcoming.

He rushed me over to the trailer, where he dropped me at the door before he sped off toward the pit.

It was a shock to see the big room full of police officers in dress uniforms watching TV. My arrival time, just like always, was at shift change, so normally there were just a few workers present, dressed in their brown overalls and boots. I wondered what was going on, but thought maybe they were watching a training film or footage that had been shot during the day with the visiting pilots.

I went to the door of our "office" to begin setting up, but the door was locked. I jiggled the handle a few times, and then I spoke into the big room, "Hey, does anybody know why this door is locked?" Several of the men turned around and looked at me with blank eyes, as if I was speaking gibberish. No one uttered a word; they all just turned back around to face the TV screen.

People acted so strangely so much of the time now that I didn't even pay much attention to this unresponsiveness. I walked slowly over to the counter on the other side of the trailer to get a cup of coffee and decided to have a bagel. Tons of food was donated daily, and the officers were starting to tease me about all the donuts I was eating. "Hey, are you sure you aren't a cop?" They would laugh as I wolfed down yet another doughnut from Dunkin' Donuts.

As I stood putting butter on the bagel, my eyes drifted up to the TV screen. At first, I couldn't mentally put together what I was looking at. When my mind placed the images, my heart leapt in my chest, and I cried out, "Oh, no! Please, no, I can't!" Once more the eyes of the police turned to look at me, but this time with some recognition of what I was feeling. Staggering, I somehow made it to a chair, where I collapsed, and then I couldn't pull my eyes away. I was looking at the inside of the World Trade Center. I realized that I was watching the video I'd heard about, but never wanted to see, the documentary *9/11*,[18] which was shot by French filmmakers during the disaster.

Sounds like rapid gunfire were exploding from the screen; in actuality, it was the jumpers as their bodies struck the ground. I was seeing the lobby of the North Tower, with FDNY and police officers standing in front of the elevator doors, looking determined but extremely upset.

I fell to pieces. It was too much. I had seen too much, tried too hard, carried too much agony from crying mothers and bereft widows, and now I had to look back to the beginning? I pulled my eyes away from the TV screen and began to look around at the officers watching the video. All the young cops had their mirrored sunglasses on so no one could see their eyes. Some of the older cops had their heads thrown back, not able to look at the screen. There were others shaking their heads back and forth, and some of them were trying not to cry.

I thought I would die before the end of the video. The last frame shown before it was over was one taken from the outside of the North Tower. Smoke was swirling around the firefighters who were going back in.

I fled from the room and held onto the railing of the porch, so sick to my stomach I thought I would vomit. Jimmy O'Hanlon was just coming around the corner toward the trailer. When he saw me, he started running and bounded onto the porch, "Raven! Are you all right?"

With tears streaming down my face, I apologized for crying.

"Please forgive me, Jimmy, I don't mean to cry. I'm really here for you guys, and you don't need to see me fall to pieces."

"Please, don't even think about apologizing to me for being the kind of good person you are," he said. With that, he handed me his handkerchief and walked off the porch, back down toward the pit.

I went back in and did Reiki on more officers that night than ever before—one after another. It was a constant flow of uninterrupted Reiki that poured through my hollowed-out core into each one of them. It's true that Reiki is a one-way street energetically, but emotionally we are human and when we are in a situation so extreme, it's difficult to guard ourselves and not soak up the emotional pain of those around us. I felt endless streams of pain, grief, and rage in the men under my hands that I was too stunned to keep from seeping into my own body.

By the time April came, those in our care had seen way too much. They were exhausted and discouraged and they couldn't wait for the work at Ground Zero to be done. Yet they were afraid of what was going to happen to them when they left and tried to return to their "regular lives."

I was working alongside Reiki master Gail Moroso, who in her early life had been a nurse in Viet Nam. "These guys are starting to remind me of the soldiers I saw on the front lines," she said. One of her regular PAPD guys had confided things in her that he was afraid to tell his commanding officers. "We are all in bad emotional shape, but we don't want to leave the mission." They were afraid that if the higher-ups found out just how badly they were feeling, they would be sent away from Ground Zero, which was the last thing they wanted. Thanks to Gail sharing this information with us, we were able to give the officers the sessions they needed without bringing up any topics we knew would upset them, or remind them of things they didn't want to think about.

April turned to May, and most of the site was cleared all the way down to the bare earth upon which the World Trade Center had once stood. We had to somehow come to grips with leaving not only Ground Zero itself, but the life we had all lived together as devotees to both the living and the dead. We knew firsthand the power of love and it was hard to let go of each other, not knowing what the road ahead even vaguely looked like. Everything we had come to know in the past eight and a half months was coming to an end.

With the removal of the last beam being slated for the morning of May 30, 2002, on the night before Ground Zero was to officially close, we came together to celebrate the end of our journey together. Some of the officers cooked hamburgers for all those who stopped by the PAPD trailer to say goodbye. It was heartwarming to see our PAPD welcoming members of the EMT, NYPD, and FDNY to their trailers, sharing hugs, handshakes, and stories. We were all finally leaving this place, this place where so many had toiled, sweated, and cried. Lieutenant Doubraski said to me, "Raven, we left our hearts in the pit. How do you live without a heart?"

I didn't have an answer, but I knew, with all the blessings that Reiki had bestowed upon this site, those hearts would be held in light.

Doing healing work in traumatic situations can change anyone. Bringing the gift of Reiki to this particular set of circumstances was not only a training ground for me, but at the same time, a blessing to the unlikely populations of the police and fire departments, who up until that time had mostly never had a traditional therapeutic massage. It was a great honor to introduce these needy individuals to something that could help them in ways that were truly meaningful and lasting. I witnessed how Reiki changed the men and women whom I worked on, while it proved itself to me in ways that would have been impossible under normal circumstances.

An important by-product of this extreme situation was that new ways were created in which Reiki can now be used by the agencies of the city, state, and US government in response to traumatic events, whether manmade or natural. There was even a proposal to the DMORT to present the idea of having Reiki practitioners accompany their teams when they are sent out on certain forensic missions.

In service to my community in this time of tragic need, I personally gained the strength in my wings that enabled me to fly.

Below is a meditation that can help you to make choices as to how things will affect you emotionally when you find yourself in a tough situation. No one can judge what is really "tough," per se. Even little things can sometimes have their own level of hurtfulness depending on how we are feeling at the time and how much power we allow those things to have over us.

We always have the power to choose, and this meditation is a great way to connect with that power of choice. This comes in handy particularly during those times when we are forced to deal with something terribly upsetting over which we have no control. This feeling of being out of control is actually an illusion; we can always decide to see things in a different way.

This is a wonderful meditation that you can do at any time. Although it will assist you when you feel like you need help, you don't need to be in distress to gain benefit from this meditation. However, for those really trying times, I recommend doing this meditation every day until you feel better.

Meditation: The Bucket of Light Meditation

Part One: Breathing Practice

This meditation can be done either sitting or lying down. Get comfortable, with your spine straight. Close your eyes; notice, as you breathe in and out, how the air passes through your nose and watch as the air goes into your lungs. If your mind sends up thoughts, think to yourself, *I wonder what my next thought will be.* This will usually still the mind, but if you are still thinking, try to simply watch your thoughts as if they are clouds passing across the sky. Begin breathing in to the count of four, hold for four counts, and exhale for eight counts. Count as fast or as slow as is comfortable for you.

Do this four-four-eight breathing pattern for ten rounds, marking the completion of each round by counting on your fingers as you complete each exhalation. Once you count out ten rounds, let your breathing return back to normal.

Part Two: Accessing Golden Light

Now imagine a beautiful, golden, sparkling light beginning to form around your head and upper body. It can look as bright as early morning or as buttery and warming as late-afternoon sunshine. Allow this glittering golden light to grow in size to surround you. The sparkles held within this light are the energies of everything positive: love, compassion, forgiveness, kindness, wholeness, tenderness, and every other wonderful thing you can think of.

Let the golden light continue to expand and extend outward, growing in size, flooding that space around you (your aura) with beautiful light. No physical object can interfere with this expansion—not walls, floors, objects, or other people. Your aura, six feet in all directions around you, is your very own, unique, and specific vibration. Allow that space to fill up with the light.

Now as you breathe in, the golden light around you is traveling on the oxygen and enters your body. The light-filled oxygen fills your lungs as you breathe.

The energy of golden light travels through your blood stream, bringing blessings to every nook and cranny of your body; it soothes you, nurtures you, and raises your vibration with every breath you take.

Notice how you feel inside as you continue to breathe in the golden light. You are whole. You are nurtured from the inside out. The golden light is the energy of living consciousness, energy full of blessings, just for you. Allow yourself to be at peace. Envision yourself glowing and vibrant. Feel inside yourself as you breathe. Know that in this very moment, you are doing everything you can to bring glorious perfection into your life. Experience yourself as happy and peaceful.

Part Three: Choosing to Fill the Bucket of Light

You are your own divine self, currently engaged in a human experience. Inside each human, there's a bucket of darkness and a bucket of light. You can tip the scales and return goodness to yourself and to the planet with the energy you create by breathing in the golden light, thereby filling your bucket of light. As you breathe in, enfold into yourself and know that you are taking very, very good care of yourself right now by breathing the light.

Watch your body breathing. Witness your human body inhaling and exhaling. Notice the witness who is watching. The witness is the real you, the divine you with ultimate power over your own life. See, hear, sense, feel, or just know the witness.

The witness says to your mind:

> *Mind, on every exhalation of breath, I command you to release all blockages, patterns, and misinformation—release any and all things that cause limitations to form and darkness to gain power over my life. On every exhalation of breath, I command you to release the matrix of thought forms and patterns and blockages that cause me pain. I command that on every exhalation of breath, all that holds me back is released from my mind, creating space for light to replace darkness.*

Let go and relax. Surrender into just breathing. Every time you exhale, you release and make a space in your mind for more light to fit in. With every breath, you empty the bucket of darkness and fill the bucket of light. Stay with this for as long as you wish, and when you are ready, come back to the present.

It is possible to conquer the past and create the future
—the first step is choosing to take the journey.

—Michele Rosenthal[19]

CHAPTER 7

Healing Mental Wounds and the Mind of PTSD

Emotions originate in the mind. The mind imagines things, and emotions follow. Because emotions can cause illness, it would be safe to say that every client I see who is ill from emotional upheaval receives Reiki healing to their mind first. This is not because I try to make things happen that way, but because Reiki is intelligent energy that automatically flows first to where it's needed the most. This is why a Reiki master can assist a person in need of mental healing. We may not know a thing about psychotherapy, but we don't need to because we are simply channeling the healing force of Reiki.

Combining Reiki sessions with psychotherapy can bring a patient back from mental distress faster than using either one of them separately. In fact, using Reiki in conjunction with any other healing modality will bring faster results. In most cases, it may seem simple and logical just to take the advice of the messengers in our current culture who are putting out books, magazine articles, films, and TV programs, all encouraging us to "think positive thoughts." This is a wonderful and remarkably effective prescription for living a healthy life under normal circumstances.

But what of the people who have lived through abnormal circumstances? I mean a traumatic event, or events, that cause the mind to be injured? Injured to the point where the person sees things that aren't really there; avoids people, certain locations, and subject matters; suffers from deep depression; or even experiences physical pain as a result of traumatization? These types of responses are known as post-traumatic stress disorder (PTSD), and through my work, I've come to believe that this condition is more prevalent in our world than is currently acknowledged.

A study was done by Dr. Naomi Breslau, the director of research at the Henry Ford Health Sciences Center's Department of Psychiatry in Detroit. She worked with eight hundred Detroit women who had experienced rape, assault, or accident and found that they all suffered from PTSD. In fact, her research further indicated that women are much more likely to experience PTSD than men.[20]

Therapist Bernice Belth has shared with me her conviction, based on her clients' reactions and studies presented by her professional colleagues, that the entire world was traumatized on September 11, 2001 and in the days after by watching things unfold on television. The human population of the earth has also experienced trauma by watching natural disasters, wars, and genocide from around the globe on our TV screens, not to mention world hunger. Here in New York City, just about everyone I know had overreactions to low-flying planes for months after the World Trade Center attack. Some even hallucinated planes crashing into buildings when obviously nothing of the sort had happened after 9/11.

In New York and in the tri-state area, PTSD was showing up in many ways in the days after the 9/11 disaster. Children were afraid to go to school and the general public had fears of trains, planes, subways, bridges, and tunnels. I notice in today's American society, many people have a tendency to shy away from talking about September 11th. One of the effects of PTSD is avoidance, so I'm not surprised. As the scenes played over and over in the twenty-four-hour news cycles, what we witnessed continuously deepened our wounds, both collectively and individually.

The only way out is through, and I shared some of my stories of trauma in chapter 6 as possible reminders of what might need to be healed within in order to move ahead in life. Storytelling has long been used by healers all over the world; bards, mystics, shamans, and spiritual teachers have, since time out of memory, told stories and used words of power to heal.

When I set out to write this book, it was my original intent to bring Reiki to war veterans as a volunteer. I discovered a precedent for providing something out of the ordinary to those who have been to war when I stumbled upon a June 7, 2004 article by *Chicago Tribune* national correspondent Kirsten Scharnberg. In her fascinating article, she tells the story of Albert Laughter, a fifth-generation Native American medicine man, employed by the federal government to help Native American vets with their PTSD from all the wars of this age: Viet Nam, the Iraq war, and Afghanistan. The article describes combining modern Western medical treatments with the ancient ceremonial healing techniques of the Native American tribal healers. As reported by Ms. Scharnberg, these non-allopathic ceremonies are restoring balance to those who have even long-standing cases of PTSD. One of the Viet Nam vets interviewed for the article stated that after years of debilitating bouts of PTSD, he was finally getting relief by using these ancient techniques.[21]

I felt this was leverage I could use to make my point that Reiki could be incorporated into the treatment of veterans. It was disappointing when my attempts to contact a decision maker at my local VA hospital went unanswered. And then my husband expressed a concern. It came while we were relaxing together in the sunshine of a beautiful summer's day. That's when he asked if I had heard back from the VA hospital. I told him that I hadn't heard yet, but that I was going to try again.

"Darling," Michael said, "I don't want you to think I'm advising you in any way, but I do have to say that I'm concerned about you working on people who have been to war."

"You are?"

"Yes, I'm the one who saw the real effects of your volunteer work after 9/11. You are still working on your own healing. I don't believe you are ready yet to handle what you will see and feel when you touch people who have witnessed the violence of war."

I felt my heart lurch and knew that he was right. Even though I knew Reiki could help, I knew I wasn't in a place to offer that assistance since I was trying to correct my own PTSD. He went on to say, "I used to know this guy who had been to Viet Nam. His best friend was blown up right next to him, and every time

I saw him, he always told me the story of how it happened. It played over and over in his mind." As Michael told me this, his eyes filled up with tears. "Even though it was his story and not mine, his pain was so great, and the telling of it was so powerful, that after a while, it was as if it had happened to me."

PTSD infects other people; it gets passed on. I knew that Michael was right. I knew I couldn't do it. Just hearing his story of something that happened long ago to somebody I never met got me crying right along with Michael in the present.

At times like this, I can always turn to my Reiki community. I was able to call William Lee Rand to ask him for a connection to another Reiki master who might have experience with veterans. Sure enough, he put me in touch with Eileen Dey, who gave me permission to share the story of one veteran from her beautiful book, *Touching the World through Reiki*. I quote just a few excerpts from a letter he wrote after attending one of the Reiki trainings Ms. Dey conducted for veterans in Seattle, Washington. This man was plagued by pain from the shrapnel that remained in his body when he was wounded in Viet Nam:

> *I wanted to pass on an overview of my pain relief results for the day. In that regard, the nerve pain in my right leg (related to a couple of old shrapnel wounds) has recently made it very hard to drive*

for any length of time, to sit in a chair for long, or to even sleep at night. Normally, sitting or driving will send me into searing pain and frequently into strong nerve flashes. Once this gets going, the only solution is multiple doses of VA prescribed pain meds ... Somehow ... through the benefits of you, Eileen, and Reiki, I made it all the way through the rest of the session, all the way home, and through the night without any other pills. That has not happened in months, and I consider it to be nothing short of a miracle.[22]

At the beginning of her nursing career, my friend and colleague, Gail Moroso, also a Reiki master and reflexologist, was stationed in Viet Nam during the war. Gail told me that many of the officers on whom we worked at Ground Zero were in the same mentally overwrought condition as the soldiers she had seen in Viet Nam. When we were getting ready to leave Ground Zero, I was sick at heart to think of the officers who wouldn't continue with any of the healing they needed. Asking for help just wasn't something most of them would consider.

I offered to continue seeing these rescue workers for free when the site closed, because I could feel how vulnerable they were to what was coming next: returning to life away from those of us who "knew." The things we knew together were all the makings of PTSD. Through being their Reiki master, I knew the things they knew. I felt those things whenever I touched them. Through them, I knew what it was like to face up to the despair of not finding the missing, not being able to bring closure to families. I knew the pain of feeling all the broken hearts lying on the ground. I knew what it was like to watch those buckets of debris leaving the site in dump trucks, carrying all that was left of people's dreams: just dust. I knew those dump trucks were taking all that was left of people's lives to Fresh Kill Landfill out on Staten Island, where police officer colleagues were manning conveyor belts, plucking out wedding rings and bones from what you had just been walking on. Yes, I brought relief to these people when they made it to my table, but how much could I transmute in twenty minutes out of a whole day, weeks, months of seeing and feeling such things? I could see that it was all just too much to carry on without getting help beyond the closing of Ground Zero.

As Gail had said all along, these people had sustained the same kind of mental injury as soldiers in war. And I was sadly correct in realizing they needed to take care of themselves in ways they weren't likely to do. There were some firefighters, police officers, and paramedics who couldn't face life anymore after all they had seen, and with all that PTSD locked inside them, decided to take matters into their own hands. I still cry with missing the ones I knew.

On September 1, 2011, a *Los Angeles Times* article entitled "9/11 Study: Multiple Health Woes Persist for Rescue Workers" described how the Mount Sinai School of Medicine in New York City had researchers that followed 27,449 emergency workers. The researchers reported that nine years after the disaster, physical and mental illnesses were still very prevalent in high percentages across a large group of 9/11 emergency responders. Of those studied, 31.9 percent had been diagnosed with PTSD. This report discusses the condition of the World Trade Center rescue, recovery, and cleanup workers and volunteers (responders) nine years after the time they spent at Ground Zero. The statistics are based on the findings of the World Trade Center Medical Monitoring and Treatment Program (WTCMMTP). This program has clinics that give free services to those who worked at Ground Zero, including the FDNY, NYPD, PAPD, paramedics, construction workers, and volunteers. They have clinics in Manhattan, Queens, Long Island, and New Jersey. Their reported findings include the following concerning PTSD:

- Among more than 11,000 firefighters in the FDNY participating in WTCMMTP nine years after 9/11, the prevalence of probably PTSD was four times higher than in the general population.
- Nine years after 9/11, rescue and recovery workers in the New York/New Jersey WTC Consortium still held high rates for PTSD (19.2

percent), depression (17.9 percent), and panic disorder (12.3 percent).

- Based on the initial screening data of nearly 21,000 rescue and recovery workers in the New York/New Jersey WTC Consortium, from 2002 to 2008, it was found that PTSD may be contributing to persisting respiratory symptoms.[23]

This last finding is truly disturbing. Many of us here in the tri-state area of New York have friends who are suffering with respiratory illnesses from breathing the air at Ground Zero. Many of these individuals also have PTSD. The findings that PTSD may be contributing to the inability to breathe properly is another major reason Reiki should be included in ongoing treatment for individuals suffering from PTSD. Not only will it help with the despair of PTSD, but imagine if it can help those who are struggling to breathe! For the police and firefighters, people more accustomed to aiding others above themselves, Reiki is a fantastic treatment option. No words are ever necessary; a person just lies down and receives its healing power of unconditional love. After all these men and women have seen, universal love may truly be the only healing remedy.

My dear friend, Gail Moroso, died from breathing that air. She was a heroine, a beautiful heart, and I miss her. If she was still here, knowing her like I did, I can just imagine she would probably be one of those nurses working in WTCMMTP, helping to make sure alternative healing modalities are available to those men and women who truly need them.

The PTSD effects of 9/11 left untreated have had disastrous effects, as was obvious in a client who came to see me two years after the tragedy.

Adam was one of the many everyday Americans who happened to be in the construction trades who volunteered at Ground Zero and then found himself with a roaring case of PTSD. Adam was an ironworker, and when he came to me, he was not able to work. He had bouts of dizziness and constant flashbacks of Ground Zero, which had caused him to fall off a building a few months prior to showing up in my office.

I knew from past experience that talking about what happened generally helped those who experienced the 9/11 trauma, and Adam allowed me to record the conversation we had before his first Reiki session, and has given his permission for me to print what he had to say, in case it can help someone else. With his eyes softening as he drifted into memory, Adam began, "I arrived at Ground Zero on September 11th around one o'clock in the afternoon." Lost in his memories, he continued, "After I saw the towers fall, I went up to my boat north of the city, and decided I was going to be needed down there at the site. I wanted to drive my boat down to the towers, but the Hudson River was closed to all traffic. Luckily, I met up with a bunch of medics who needed transportation down the river, so I got through by driving them down to Chelsea Piers where I docked my boat. Then I jumped into a truck with a bunch of other iron-workers and we went down to the towers."

Adam went on to explain that he stayed at the Ground Zero site for two months without leaving, sleeping on cots and eating meals provided by the Red Cross. After weeks of backbreaking work, in spite of feeling guilty about taking time for himself, he finally broke down to receive some of the healing services being offered by volunteers on the floating triage center set up on a boat in the Hudson River, close to the site. As our conversation continued, I got a bird's-eye view into the hearts and minds of the amazing construction workers who helped out.

"Adam, were the therapists you saw from New York?"

"They were from all over. I can't remember exactly, but I just remember there were massage therapists of all kinds everywhere. It was unbelievable. I couldn't believe my eyes."

"Did it make it easier for you to do your job, feeling like you were surrounded by people who cared about you?"

"Oh, absolutely."

"I would imagine that you were being asked to help firefighters who were looking for their friends. Did you ever feel emotionally spent?"

"Yeah, but I kinda like … numbed myself to it, ya know? It was more than a big demo job. It was a job with a purpose of, unfortunately, having to hopefully find some live people, and it happened a couple of times, but not that much. So I forget how many days went by. Time-wise, it felt like one long day for me. There were firefighters and rescue workers from all over the country on the pile with these long wands that would hear heartbeats thirty feet down, and you could tell they were losing hope. But they just kept going."

"Did you ever find any people?"

Adam whispered, "Yeah. Yeah. I mean, I didn't personally find them, but I was there when they were body-bagging them and I passed a lot of people down in the bucket brigade thing they had. I was in a spot, it must have been a spot where a lot of people were, because it would be like, bucket, bucket, bucket, body bag, bucket, bucket, body bag, and then after a while, you'd be passing down a body bag, and it would feel empty. It was probably just a small piece of somebody in there."

"There are so many memories. Is it hard to deal with them?"

"Yeah, it's heavy duty."

"Do you feel that you experienced extra stress because you never found people alive?"

"It was a bummer. For me, there was a lot of doubt about voids. There was always that feeling that we weren't doing enough. But they weren't letting civilians crawl into holes. The chiefs and captains of the fire department wouldn't let regular people like me crawl under debris."

"Were you aware of the fact that everybody at Ground Zero felt like they weren't doing enough?"

"Yeah, we were thinking, *God, what are we doing?* In the beginning, it was frustrating because we didn't have cranes. We didn't have booms to get far enough over. We had to work the debris out in order to get the cranes in."

"Do you operate a crane?"

"No, no, I'm an ironworker. That's a different trade. They're the operating engineers. I felt bad for the operating engineers, I really did. Especially the guys who operated the grabbers, because the grabber guys would grab a beam and they'd hear, 'All right, hold up!' and a torso or something would be removed, or another part or a piece of something. Those guys, oh boy, they had to feel bad, especially in the beginning, because they were grabbing at things with these big machines, and they must have felt like maybe they killed some people by accident. My heart goes out to the operating engineers, because they had a lot of that stuff going on."

"Now that we're two years beyond what happened there, are you working on your healing?"

"I'm trying to. I still have sad feelings."

"Are you planning on expanding the healing techniques that you will use?"

"Yeah, right now. Right now I'm in the Reiki room. I'll try anything. I do think about Ground Zero every day. I never saw that kind of stuff before, and it was shocking. I ask myself, *Why don't I just get on with my life and forget about all this?* I'd love to forget this happened, but I can't. So when my friend calls me out of the blue to tell me about Reiki, well here I am, trying to get better by having Reiki for the first time."

Adam had a very serious case of PTSD. He trusted me enough to release on my table by crying through most of that first session, until the very end, when he fell asleep. When it was over, his equilibrium seemed to be restored, and he was amazed by how good he was feeling. Adam came for sessions a few more times. When he got to a place of feeling much better, we kept in touch via phone calls here and there, with me sometimes sending him Reiki remotely.

I believe PTSD is more common than we acknowledge in our culture. It's just beginning to be understood as an underlying cause of many types of psychiatric illnesses. New studies show that PTSD is often at the bottom of depression and alcoholism, especially in women.

For myself, I know firsthand what it's like to have PTSD. I had a pretty bad case of it myself after the eight and a half months of my volunteer Reiki work following

September 11th. PTSD first started to reveal itself in me after I saw the film *9/11*. Right after my volunteer shift that night, I was scheduled to teach a meditation class at one of the Equinox clubs. I was running late, so I was driven to the snazzy downtown club in a police car. Once inside, I stopped in the ladies' locker room to splash some water on my tired face. In a daze, and almost in slow motion, I lifted my face from the sink and began to watch the models and actresses primping their hair in front of the mirrors, listening to them complain about lipstick brands. It was too much for me—such starkly different realities were crashing into each other inside me. I felt like I was going to throw up. I had just been looking into the jaws of hell, helping broken people to keep going, and now I was looking into gleaming, high-society mirrors with lipstick conversations around me. *Crash. Crash. Crash.* I could feel the crashing inside ... the horror of the video, the way it affected us all, was all crashing, crashing, crashing. I was filled to the top with emotions too strong to handle anymore.

I made my way into the studio where I was scheduled to teach guided meditation and just sat down on the floor. I knew I couldn't do it. There is a rule at Equinox that if no one comes to your class for ten minutes past its starting time, you can leave. I never, ever in all my life had that happen to me, but it happened now. It was as if the angels were watching over me. There was no way I could guide anybody anywhere except to a place they'd never want to go. After the ten minutes were up, I started crying. Out of nowhere, my fitness manager flew into the studio and held me in her arms as I cried. With great compassion and care, she helped me out of the building and into a taxi.

I don't remember the ride home at all; I just remember coming through my apartment door, crying so hard I could hardly stand up. I saw my husband's face shock white as he caught me in his arms and put me to bed. I stayed there for three days and nights, shivering from the visions of all I had seen over the months flashing behind my eyes, and crying endlessly. I couldn't eat because I was crying. I couldn't sleep because I was crying. I couldn't do anything but lie there and wonder if I would ever stop crying again. The pain inside me was unbelievable.

Michael called the Ground Zero site coordinator, Linda Hazlett, who by now was my dear friend, to tell her I was in bed in really bad shape and that I wouldn't be showing up for my shifts at Ground Zero in the foreseeable future. Linda called other healers to let them know that one of us had gone down. People began calling me, not just from New York, from all over the country, praying with me over the phone, souls I never met and whose names I will never remember. But the worst was yet to come.

After three days of crying, I was too exhausted to continue. The tears just stopped. Michael took this as a good sign. He was so relieved, and he decided to take our darling Vizsla girl, Echo, out for a walk.

I felt like I needed to be in water, so I ran a bath. When I got into the bathtub, I left the hot water faucet running just a bit so I would stay very warm, and the *drip*, *drip*, *drip* became hypnotic. My mind started wandering, going over all the things I had seen over the long months, matching them to things I saw on the video. I felt the pain of the mothers I had held, the children who were now orphans, and the men and women who had lost their spouse. The tears started up again—only this time I was screaming. I was screaming, and something terrifying had crept up that I never saw before. The blackness was so dark that I wanted to die. I just didn't want to live in a world where people flew planes into buildings, where everyone died, and hearts were broken beyond fixing... I screamed and screamed, and then I began to hear something in between my screams. The voice of Gabriel was crying out to me, *Never underestimate the power of the Light!*

Scream.

Never underestimate the power of the Light!

Scream.

Never underestimate the power of the Light!

Finally, I could feel what the voice was saying. I could feel the love that was surrounding me and washing through me, the love that my Reiki master angel was beaming into me, the Reiki love that is divine. I felt myself drinking it in, deeper and deeper into my heart, my mind, my cells … It was the end and the beginning. It was the beginning of my true healing, and my becoming what I am today, but it would be quite a long journey back to wholeness, and on that afternoon in my bathtub, the journey was in its infancy.

I'm sharing this story for three very important reasons:

1. No matter how bad things get, there is always more love coming down the road to save you;
2. No matter how bad things get, life can still turn into something beautiful; and
3. No matter how bad things get, there is still time to take care of yourself, which will turn everything around and make it better.

In the months following September 11th, a great number of us didn't realize those three things. Survivor guilt was rampant and many surely didn't know that we should, or even could, take care of ourselves. Nor did we ever imagine we would have a beautiful life again, although I believe many of us felt the protection of divine spirits and angels, even if we weren't always totally conscious of it.

In the months that followed the closing of the Ground Zero site, I lived the nightmare of seeing things that weren't really there. It's unnerving to know you are walking around with the possibility of being thrown into horrible emotions that seem out of your control without a moment's notice to prepare. I have been stunned to see the pit of Ground Zero form in front of my eyes as I casually glanced into a construction site I was walking by in uptown Manhattan. I have shockingly seen Ground Zero appear in a TV commercial when a truck stopped short at the rim of the Grand Canyon. I have seen the devastation of September 11th all around me when a piece of paper wafted through the air over the street in my neighborhood. I have burst into tears, hearing the buildings fall in the roaring sound of the express subway train racing by. When I've experienced these things, the pit of my stomach has gone into a terrible stress feeling more awful than anything I can begin to describe.

In my case, I was brought back to myself through giving myself Reiki (which is learned in Reiki training), receiving Reiki treatments from others, continuing to give Reiki treatments to others (when giving a session, Reiki practitioners also receive the benefits as though receiving a session), and immersing myself in regular talk therapy. I had never had a psychotherapist in my life before September 11th, but I definitely needed a lot of help with my own healing once the cleanup of Ground Zero was concluded.

PTSD was a constant worry for those who worked at Ground Zero. There were reports in the newspapers about how some of the rescue and recovery workers had roaring cases of it, testament by that fact being that they were forgetting regular things (like paying bills), or in some severe cases, even forgetting where they lived. The PAPD officers had been down there from day one. During the time when we were getting closer to the closing of the site, my friend Jimmy O'Hanlon said to me, "Raven, nobody can tell us what will happen to us. Nobody's been through this kind of thing before. Nobody ever had to dig for people over such a long period of time. We really don't know what to expect..."

When I spoke on this subject with FDNY Captain Gormley, he had this to say:

> *We wanted mandated counseling, mandated examinations for every guy in our house... I wanted to know what happened to the tracking of the guys who were from the same battalion that survived the 101st Airborne crash in Canada. That crash took out a couple of infantry companies and there were survivors who knew them. They went up there and they dug them out. What happened to those guys down the road?... What happened to the rest of the guys that went digging out the 241 Marines in Beirut that got killed by the truck bomb when the building collapsed? Were those guys tracked? How were they treated? Those were similar events.*[24]

When I prayed to help the PAPD with getting their hearts back, as I had promised Lieutenant Doubraski I would, Gabriel told me that the solution given would help with the healing of their PTSD. As I sat in prayer and meditation, Gabriel gave the following ceremony:

> *Find a container into which the men can place a token of value to them that will be left at Ground Zero in place of their hearts. Help them to concentrate on calling their hearts back to them when they place their objects into the container. Tell them the container will become part of Ground Zero when the container is placed in the cement when it is poured.*

Because the PAPD were still in charge of the site, it was possible to have the container put into the cement. So the ceremony given by Gabriel took place in August of 2002 under the famous cross that was found in the rubble. It was wonderful to see Lieutenant Doubraski and all the other officers arriving from their posts. To begin, I called in the angels, throwing rose petals onto Ground Zero. Lightning flashed and thunder roared as a sudden cleansing rain gently washed over us. Then, one by one, the officers put their treasures into a fairytale-looking gourd the shape and size of a smallish pumpkin sent to us by the kahuna (spiritual priests) of Hawaii. The kahuna had graced the bottom of the gourd with stones from the most sacred land in all of the Hawaiian Islands. Everyone had tears in their eyes as they put their objects into the gourd. I touched one Reiki-filled hand to each chest, instructing them, "Call your heart back. Feel love pour into you. Be whole and go forward and bring blessings to all who know you. By being whole, you honor your brothers and sisters who died here. They are depending on you to heal and to remember and to take care of those they left behind."

There are no words with which to describe this kind of Reiki healing power. I will never forget it.

And what about people just like you who have had personally upsetting experiences that are not being recognized as trauma, like those who have had traumatic experiences in hospitals, for example? How many times have you heard someone say, "I hate hospitals"? Why do you think that is? And what is anyone doing about *that* type of PTSD? I've had long discussions on this subject with Luana DeAngelis, founder and president of You Can Thrive. She tells me that all the women afflicted with breast cancer who come to receive services in her organization have PTSD. They are traumatized every time they touch a hospital door.

Reiki has proven to be a preventive to PTSD for those going through breast cancer. For the women I've led through cancer treatments and surgeries, I can honestly say they have not experienced PTSD from having undergone their lifesaving allopathic cancer treatments, no matter how difficult their processes have been. This is huge. Reiki helps prevents trauma from nestling itself within a person's psyche and inner being; this being the case, a woman is much more likely to see her care all the way through to the end of what her doctors recommend, rather than balk and turn away from the treatments that can save her life.

Please acknowledge the places in your life where PTSD might dwell. Has there been someone you love who has died in a difficult way? Have you witnessed a motor vehicle accident that traumatized you? Did something happen to you when you were a child that you might not even remember consciously, but continue to have dreams about? Are there reoccurring patterns of thought that produce bad feelings for you? Note them, and love yourself enough to do something to heal. You deserve to be happy. We all do.

To everyone out there who has suffered a trauma of any kind, if you didn't get help after it happened, and you're still thinking about it, please get some help now. You deserve to be happy, healthy, and operating at the highest level of your abilities—for your own sake, and the sake of everyone you encounter. Reiki can definitely help. If you don't presently know anyone to go to for Reiki, what follows is a meditation you can use in the meantime. This meditation can be used to help you with any PTSD in your life, regardless of the traumatic event. I recommend that you do this meditation with your journal and a pen close by so you can record what happened once you are done.

Guided Meditation: PTSD Meditation and Becoming an Instrument of Healing Power

Part One: PTSD Meditation

Bring your awareness to your breathing. Notice the air passing across the tips of your nostrils. Bring your awareness deep into the center of your chest and watch yourself breathing. You are breathing all the time, but now you are the witness. Just watch ... Call Archangels Ariel, Raphael, Michael, and Gabriel, asking them to surround you with golden light that extends six feet around you in all directions. This light is uninterrupted by walls, floors, or other people.

You become aware that you are breathing in this golden light from the air around you. The light is in the air as it enters your lungs and travels through your body. Notice that the light you are breathing in is filled with feelings of love. This love flows through your veins, healing you physically, emotionally, mentally, and spiritually—healing every part of you. Surrender to being healed by the light. It is the healing light of the angels.

See, hear, sense, feel, or just know this healing angelic light coalescing into a star in the center of your chest.

Intend or pretend (whichever works best for you) that you are opening the top of your head to receive a stream of light from the highest realms of divinity (you can call it God, Goddess, All That Is, whatever feels right to you). You are opening the crown of your head to receive a direct connection to the divine. Let this flow into you as a stream of brilliant light that runs from the top of your head down through your whole body.

Ask for healing of all that hurt you (the loss of your loved one, witnessing an accident, September 11, 2001 and afterward, or any other traumas that require healing). Ask for the healing to be in your body, mind, emotions, and spirit. Take as much time as you need. Don't rush it.

Go back to that star in the center of your chest. Notice that it is now full of a mixture of light—the golden light of the angels is mixed with the brilliant white light of the divine. Move your awareness into that star of light in your chest and see, hear, sense, feel, or just know as it begins to grow in size, larger and larger, until it expands to fill the whole room or space.

Absorb the light from the space around you in through your skin. Surrender to being healed deeply, deeper and deeper with each passing second.

You can end the meditation here, if you wish.

Part Two: Becoming an Instrument of Healing Power

If you always wanted to do something to help after any traumatic event to which you've been connected, or if you experienced a tragic event and always wished you could have helped more, you can do so now by staying in the light and holding the intention to become an instrument of its goodness and healing power.

With your intention, will, prayer, and wish to help, bring your awareness to the huge ball of light that fills the room or space. Envision this huge ball of light you have made, infused with the loving power of angels and divinity, rise up into the sky. Watch it travel toward the location where your traumatic event took place, growing in size as it moves along its course. All you have to do is intend; the angels do the rest to carry the light.

See, hear, sense, feel, or just know the ball of light arriving and beginning to settle around the area, surrounding it in light that extends miles down into the earth, miles high into the skies above, and miles out in all directions. Call to the angels and the ancestors; call whomever or whatever your heart tells you to call, asking for the healing of everyone and everything that was affected by the event, including your own Self.

Call in blessings to replace tragedy, love to replace grief, and healing to replace pain. Take as long as you need to feel complete.

Thank everything and everyone who assisted you with this healing. Leave the light there as you bring your awareness back to your own heart. Notice that your body is full of light and that your own aura, extending six feet out in all directions, continues to be filled with golden light.

Notice that you are breathing. Give thanks yet again. Watch yourself breathe. When you are ready, open your eyes.

I recommend that you write as much as you can remember in your journal. The writing can be your own private "telling." I recommend doing this meditation more than once. In fact, you could do it as a special kindness to yourself for your own healing as much as you feel you need or want to. If you have the time, it would be ideal to do it once daily from a new moon to the next full moon to add the healing power of nature to your experiences.

I have been born more times
than anybody except Krishna.
—*Mark Twain*[25]

CHAPTER 8

Healing the Spirit: Reiki and Life after Death

While our discussion has largely been on the effect of Reiki on the physical, mental, and emotional levels, I would now like to expand the conversation to the mystical side of Reiki, which helps in understanding the vast reach of its healing power. In times of loss, Reiki is such a balm to our hearts; we have all lost loved ones to death, and although it is so hard to say good-bye to them as we continue to be in life without them, Reiki has the power to show those who are grieving that life is eternal.

I've already shared with you the first time I met the spirit of a loved one, the father of my client named Calvin. Over time, I accepted this gift of communication with those on the other side and how it presented itself when I would offer Reiki. It didn't scare me or bother me at all like it might others. Each time I was a little less surprised, and gradually more excited to share messages that had a profound effect on those meant to hear them. And since that first time, I've learned that a Reiki master doesn't even need to be in the same room with a client in order to receive information from a deceased family member.

Andrea came to me because her sister was dying of cancer. Utterly heartbroken, she felt certain that if she enrolled in my course to become a Reiki master, she'd be able to help heal, and possibly even cure her sister, Sarah, who had made the decision early on that she didn't want to battle her illness using traditional Western medicine. It was Sarah's personal decision that she wanted to use only natural and alternative medical practices to treat her stage-IV cancer.

As I began working with Andrea, guiding her through the levels of Reiki training, we talked a lot about her sister along the way. Then Andrea came to see me one afternoon, very upset, with news that was troubling to her. She explained to me that Sarah loved having Reiki sessions, but her illness was not subsiding. I was terribly sorry for her pain, but felt it necessary to explain.

"Reiki always goes where it is needed and will work on whatever healing needs to occur—it cannot be forced to do something that goes against the higher will of the person you are treating. Sometimes the healing that is needed is much different from what we imagine. Sometimes the healing is to help a person to die." Although it was difficult information for her to hear, it was an important thing for her to know.

We do not control Reiki; if you decide you are going to make someone better, then your ego is involved. Our intention should always be to bring healing, whatever that truly means for the person in our care. This can be difficult emotionally when the person you are treating is a beloved relative, yet if you truly understand this in advance, the Reiki sessions you share with the beloved can bring you closer to that person. I had the experience of quietly giving Reiki to my own mother in her last moments before death. From that experience, I can tell you this: it is a great honor and privilege to be with someone when they pass into the next world, and Reiki is an amazing gift to be able to share at that time. As a matter of fact, there is a body of Reiki practitioners who do just that: assist the dying in hospices throughout the country. Their work is very rewarding for them personally, and a very big help to all concerned.

In the case of Andrea and her sister, some time went by and I was gearing up to hold another Reiki training when I heard that Sarah had just passed away. Not sure in what other way I could help, I called Andrea and offered to do a distance treatment on her sister to help ease her transition into the spirit realm.

You might be thinking, *Reiki to a dead person? But they don't even have a body!* The truth is that to be "alive" or to be "dead" are human terms. And as such, they only apply to our very human world. Here on earth we are born, we grow old, and then we eventually die. But in reality, there is no end to our lives.

Having received Andrea's permission to do the distance treatment, I sat quietly and called out to Sarah's spirit to come to me so that I could offer her the Reiki session. I felt her presence come as a wash of warmth in the air before me. I'd never met her in life, but now I could feel her. She had a very sweet and peaceful presence. I asked her to lie down before me so that I could administer Reiki. (A spirit, when it's receiving Reiki, presents itself as an exact—but etheric—duplicate of the last physical body.) I could feel her energy, just like there was a living person there, under my hands. But the moment after Sarah settled down before me, I felt a terrible fluttering of anxiety. Her energy completely changed.

What's bothering you? Why are you so upset? I asked. Like Calvin's father, Sarah communicated her thoughts by projecting them directly into my mind.

She was incredibly distraught over her family's reaction to her death. She told me that they were not only feeling torn apart by the loss, but battling terrible guilt. They had respected her wishes to handle her disease using natural medicine, but now that she had died, they worried they should have done more—been sterner in response to her decision, made her go through surgeries, chemotherapy, etc. She didn't want her family to worry over whether they should have forced her to use traditional Western treatments, especially when that wasn't what she had wanted.

I chose to die, she told me adamantly.

But why? I wondered. *Why would you choose to die?*

Sarah seemed amused that I would ask, and explained that for her soul's growth and education, she was seeking information, an experience, that for her was like a piece to a puzzle. It was a piece in the puzzle of existence concerning life and death.

For Sarah, dying was the only way she could get the answer she was looking for. This can be a pretty tough idea for the living to swallow, but it's important to understand that Sarah was truly happy to have gained the knowledge she'd been looking for. As a matter of fact, she was in bliss! She only wanted her family to stop suffering over the choice she had made.

At that point, it dawned on me what the issue with her treatment had been.

As a person, Sarah had agreed to the treatment. But her *spirit* didn't desire for the treatments to heal her physically because her spirit wanted to experience death. Nothing Andrea, or anybody else for that matter, could have done would have made any difference. The alternative and natural treatments Sarah chose provided the comfort she needed to receive her true healing in death.

I understand, I told Sarah. *I promise I'll tell your sister*.

In response, I got an image of Sarah's spirit turning into a beautiful white dove beneath my hands. As the dove filled with blinding light, she began to slowly stretch open her wings. When the tips of the wings met over her head, she turned into beams of brilliant light, streaming out in all directions until she disappeared. I'd never experienced anything like it. The room felt filled with a shimmering, glittery light.

I waited, curiously listening. Gabriel whispered to me, *We have her; she is safe and happy with us*, and I knew that her adventures in the new phase of her life had just begun.

As the light slowly faded and I became present again in the room, I touched my fingers to my cheek to find my face was soaked with tears. Blowing my nose, I pulled myself together and dialed Andrea right away. As I told her the story, she wept so hard I started to apologize—I'd really put my foot in it this time. I hadn't meant to make matters worse! But Andrea just laughed.

"Raven, no, please, don't feel bad. I'm just crying because I feel so much relief. All the doubting and guilt—it's all we've been talking about since Sarah passed away."

The next night I called again at Andrea's request and related my experience for the rest of family on speakerphone. Although they were still shattered with grief, Andrea later told me that they hung on every word of Sarah's message. The fact that Sarah had found the answer she was seeking, and that wherever she might be, she felt blissful and at peace didn't change that Sarah's family missed her terribly. But the relief they felt was palpable, and the guilt went away. Now they knew that Sarah was happy, and they wanted her to be able to look down on them and, instead of seeing their hurt and pain, see a reflection of her gift in the lives they were living for themselves.

We can examine death all we want, talk about it until we're blue in the face, but it will never get any easier. The truth of the matter is that dying is much harder on the living than it is for those who are dead. We are left with the life-sized voids, the memories, the remnants, the longing. It could almost seem cruel that our loved ones have moved on without us. Or that they've left us, even though we loved them so. But through my spiritual and Reiki practice I have come to better understand this as a necessary (albeit very challenging) part of our development. Just as there is no single one of us with the same fingerprint as another on this entire planet, each and every soul is utterly unique. Each of us comes into this world with our own path we must walk, a path that belongs solely to us. We each have our own experiences that we seek to make ourselves whole in whatever areas we are spiritually lacking. Experience is what life is all about, and for this reason and so many others, life is such an incredible gift. When we begin to understand that life is a never-ending experience, a journey, we begin to see that the best thing we can do is to live our lives joyfully.

My friend Amy's sister was expecting a baby, and so Amy was planning to go to Portland, Oregon to be there in time for her niece's birth. I was shocked to get a call from Amy a few nights before her scheduled trip. She was sobbing, completely distraught, asking me if I could please send Reiki to the newly born baby girl. She'd received word that the baby's health was at terrible risk due to complications. She couldn't give me any specific details because she herself had just found out; no one knew very much at that point.

I hung up the phone right away and, sitting quietly, reached out to the baby's spirit.

Baby girl, niece of Amy, please come to me so that I might assist you. The baby's response was immediate—I felt her spirit in the room right away. As I began the Reiki session, I felt great trauma in the baby's head and even more distress in her chest. But these problems were strictly physical; the baby herself was very calm, even serene. I was administering Reiki to the newborn when I heard something utterly unmistakable in my mind:

Stop.

She wanted me to stop? But I'd felt her clearly give me permission before I began. Worried and more than a little confused, I immediately ceased.

What's going on? I asked. *Why do you want me to stop?*

I want you to stop because I haven't made up my mind, she told me. *Right now I'm deciding whether I want to stay, or whether I want to go back.*

This was completely new territory for me. Whether it was because of the injury she'd suffered, or whether she just wasn't ready to start life on earth at this time, it seemed that the Reiki she'd received had helped her decide something. She showed me a long hallway, and at both ends I could see lighted doorways. I understood what she was trying to say: there was no "right" or "wrong"—there was only a choice to be made. The choice was hers alone.

I ended the treatment, but not before sending her love and wishing her all the luck in the universe with whichever decision she made. To learn that we each "choose" was one of the greatest gifts I've received as a Reiki master. A few minutes later, I called Amy and told her everything, sorry that I didn't have more definitive news. The next morning I learned that the baby had made her choice during the night; she had passed away. It was a horrible, wrenching experience for the newborn girl's family. But knowing that the baby had been so peaceful, that she herself had made the decision to go "back into the light" was a comfort to both the baby's mother and to Amy. Two years later, Amy's sister got pregnant again, and this time the pregnancy was without complications. She gave birth to a robust and healthy little girl.

I still think about that newborn little girl who went back into the light and send her love. Though it was horribly sad and painful for all who were involved, she gifted us with a glimpse of the inner workings of our existence that I would go on to use in helping more clients heal, and to understand how we all come to be on this planet in the first place.

When my friend, Allison, who was a great healer herself, died unexpectedly, the despair her friends felt was mixed with utter shock. Allison was a twenty-nine-year-old woman when she contracted an infection. She had healed so many people in her career as an acupuncturist, and everyone was completely knocked off-kilter by her death. Allison had succumbed to her infection in a hospital, with only her mother present. She had a boyfriend who adored her, who was absolutely heartbroken.

I, too, was very close to Allison. She had taken Reiki training with me all the way to Master Level. I had visited her for her legendary acupuncture treatments, spiced with Reiki. After she died, her spirit was reaching out to me. I could feel and hear her asking me for distance Reiki. On the afternoon following her memorial service, I sat down to comply with her wish.

Allison came to me as she had looked in life, but surrounded by white light. It seemed as though the light was in her and all around her at the same time. She was smiling as she looked at me. As we got going with the Reiki session, she asked me to heal her emotions concerning her sadness to leave her family, and especially her boyfriend. Allison kept up a conversation with me via silent communication. Our thoughts were flowing easily between us. She told me that she would be sending someone else to be with her boyfriend, whom she loved so much, and that she herself was moving on to fulfill a dream that had always lived in her deepest heart: to heal children. In physical life, she hadn't had that opportunity, but now she would be able to help lots of kids all at once. She didn't give me any other details about how she would be doing this; she just shared that she loved me, which I knew. When the session was over, she smiled and beamed love to me as she disappeared. I was able to share this information with one of Allison's best friends. I left it up to her to decide whether or not to tell Allison's parents and her boyfriend, as I didn't know them personally.

For Calvin, the ophthalmologist whose father had died in a difficult way, Reiki helped him to have faith in life after death, and also helped to heal some of the grief trapped in his body over the loss of his father. In the cases of Sarah and the peaceful infant girl, Reiki enabled them to cross over to the next phase of their journey. And for Andrea, Reiki helped her understand that Reiki goes where it is needed; it cannot be directed. To do so is to force your will upon another, and there's simply no way we can do this when we're dealing with the spiritual world! Souls are going to do what they need to do.

The fact of the matter is that none of us has the right to interfere with anyone's spiritual progress, no matter how much we love them. It's a principle of Reiki, but it is also a universal law that comes down to us from the very highest levels of existence. No one has the right to make a decision for anyone else when it comes to their personal path, and living and dying are a part of that spiritual journey. Who are we to insist that someone live when their path really involves experiencing something else?

Sarah's family couldn't force her to seek treatment for her cancer in ways she didn't want. If they had interfered, they would have created or manifested more trouble down the line, for themselves as well as for Sarah. It could have manifested as bankruptcy due to exorbitant hospital bills, family feuding, or simply prolonged suffering for Sarah.

My point is: all we can ever do is love people. We can let them know we're there, that we want to help, and then be there if they ask us. This in itself can be incredibly difficult, especially when it comes to depression, self-imposed loneliness, or drug addiction. When people feel compelled to go down a certain path, believe me, they are going to head down that path, whether you want them to or not. We can try to stop them, give them slaps on the wrist and say, "Don't do that." But in the end, they are here to learn their own lessons in their own ways and in their own time. No matter what we might think, I've come to see that if a soul doesn't truly want to make a change, it just can't happen.

On the other hand, if somebody wants to make their life better, we're here for that. Reiki practitioners can channel the universal energy and restore balance so people can continue to grow. But sometimes the greatest act of love of all is to let somebody fall. You might be able to see it coming, clear as a bell, but there isn't a damn thing you can do about it other than to love them.

What helps us let go when we need to is the understanding that the spirit of a person does go on. And no matter what, it is our love for one another that truly endures. Love outlasts everything.

Guided Prayer: Praying to Your Reiki Master in Spirit for Healing

It's true that you must get a person's permission before you do a healing on them. It's also true that you can pray for people without their permission; it's done all the time, every day all over the world. What I present here is a way to use prayer to your Reiki master in spirit to ask for healing.

Once you have connected with your Reiki master in spirit, you can begin to pray for the healing of yourself, your family members, your friends, or anyone else in need. You can also use this prayer technique to ask for the healing of anyone you know who is deceased.

Sit quietly for a few moments, and if possible, light a candle. Close your eyes and call your Reiki master in spirit. Take as much time as you need to connect in your own way, whether that is to see, hear, sense, feel, or just know that your Reiki master in spirit has come to join you. Once you have the experience of connection, communicate what is going on. Give the name of whomever you are praying for, even if it's yourself, and explain what the problem is. You can project all this information to your Reiki master in spirit directly from your mind and heart, or you can whisper everything out loud if that makes it easier for you. Then simply ask your Reiki master in spirit for whatever healing is needed. Continue to sit in silence. You can decide ahead of time if you are going to spend a certain amount of time doing this, or whether you are going to end when you feel you are done.

It can be very emotional as your heart opens during the prayer session, so be gentle with yourself. Don't worry if you cry—that's quite common and normal to have a profound reaction to being in the presence of such a beautiful being of light. For as long as you are in the presence of your Reiki master in spirit, continuously emanate *Thank you, thank you, thank you* out of your heart. When you feel ready, open your eyes.

Now you must trust. Remember that everyone has their own choices to make when it comes to their personal healing. You have done your best and given the greatest love you can give. Trust in that.

Reputation is what men and women think of us;
character is what God and angels know of us.

—*Thomas Paine*[26]

CHAPTER 9

Reiki in the Modern World

Reiki is a path proven to change everything that it touches into something better. It brings beauty because it is beautiful. It brings peace because it is peaceful. It brings joy because it is joyful and it brings love because it is unconditional love.

You've now seen the ways in which Reiki has been used effectively in the twenty years of my practice. It is a balm to those who are facing severe medical procedures, including surgeries. It helps those with cancer to withstand their chemotherapy and radiation treatments. It brings relief to people suffering from PTSD. It can be a saving grace in the face of traumatic events. It brings healing of physical injuries to professional athletes. It heals the spirit of the living after the loss of a loved one, and can be used to help the deceased.

In modern society, what I witness is an overall malaise and disconnection from Self that causes many kinds of dis-ease. No matter what the cause, I continue to notice that many of those who face serious illnesses are often being made sick by something deep within themselves, something that is longing to get on the path to their right destiny. The world is now populated by amazing souls—souls that carry the power to bring more love back to the earth. Of those in my care, I have witnessed time and again a deep need to do good works and to fulfill a destiny that is longing to come out into the light of day.

I live in a city of wealth where millionaires populate every neighborhood and material abundance seems to be the rule rather than the exception. Yet what I experience in this wealthy population is the kind of unhappiness that comes from being disconnected from what is really important. As you have seen in these pages, Reiki can open doors within you and bring you to where you were always meant to be... the place you chose for yourself, a place filled with healing, happiness, fulfillment, love, and true prosperity.

The reason I believe Reiki can change the world we live in is twofold. First, it strengthens any other healing modality or practice it might be used in combination with, like yoga, massage, meditation, and so on. Second, when a person is working with Reiki, either as a receiver or as a giver of this beautiful energy, it positively affects their internal vibration, much like a tuning fork affects the vibration of a person or object it is placed upon. This higher vibration of love affects everyone and everything a person comes in contact with. So whether you are a doctor, lawyer, stockbroker, soldier, sister, wife, mother, and so on, you begin to effect change around you through your high vibration. Beyond that, to those drawn to practice Reiki, to become a Reiki practitioner is a joy beyond words. It means you administer the power that transforms darkness into light.

When one continues to stand in the flow of Reiki, doorways of perception begin to open. One can be blessed with sight into other beautiful realms of existence if it is chosen by free will to experience them. In my case, as I started to heal from the PTSD, Reiki brought my healing into ever-expanding love.

The more I do Reiki, the more I get to experience how powerful it is! For example, after giving Reiki to all the trees by our country house before a recent hurricane, they all stood strong in the winds that tore down trees on every other property around us. With so much true loving power available to us, what can possibly stand in the way of fulfilling one's destiny? My deepest prayer is that this book will open doors for Reiki in our modern world, and that the Reiki practitioners in this world can bring their beautiful works to the people who need them.

With the support of doctors like Feldman and Oz, I envision a time in the (hopefully) not-too-distant future when Reiki will be used much more widely in medicine. I look forward to the days ahead, when it is part of the care of professional athletes so they can go on to enjoy their lives pain-free once their careers are over. I can imagine Reiki being administered extensively at sites of natural disasters. And without a doubt, it will continue to be incorporated into hospice care to guide those who are crossing over into the light.

I believe these hopes and dreams depend on our uniting together in dedication to love and to making the world a better place. The best part in all of us is the part that longs to do good things. The pure and simple road of Reiki can get you on that path, or strengthen the path you're already on.

To any of you who may presently be ill, or facing a very big challenge, I hope you will take heart from what I have shared and realize that no matter how bad your own personal struggles might be right now, you can still find your way to a healthy, happy, and beautiful life. You already have it in you to be a vessel of love, because that beautiful "something" is right there inside you, unfolding its wings even as you read these words. In spite of everything I have seen and lived through, beauty continues to expand within my life, revealing ever more wonders every day. I credit this joyous unfolding to finding Reiki. Perhaps it would be more accurate to say that Reiki found me, just like it may be finding you right now.

To conclude, I'd like to speak directly to your heart, my treasured reader, to say I believe that you and I are part of a family of light-bearers who show up, like King Arthur, when we are needed, no matter where that is in the universe. I believe that you and I have waited a very long time to be here together at this exact moment. I hold out my hand to you, my dear old friend, with deep joy in my heart. Blessings upon you, no matter what trail you may take. May the path shine brightly beneath your feet and bring you happiness and love.

Guided Meditation: Awaken Your Personal Quest

Part One: Breathing Practice

This meditation can be done either sitting or lying down. Get comfortable, with your spine straight. Close your eyes; notice, as you breathe in and out, how the air passes through your nose and watch as the air goes into your lungs. If your mind sends up thoughts, think to yourself, *I wonder what my next thought will be.* This will usually still the mind, but if you are still thinking, try to simply watch your thoughts as if they are clouds passing across the sky. Begin breathing in to the count of four, hold for four counts, and exhale for eight counts. Count as fast or as slow as is comfortable for you.

Do this four-four-eight breathing pattern for ten rounds, marking the completion of each round by counting on your fingers as you complete each exhalation. Once you count out ten rounds, let your breathing return back to normal.

Part Two: Accessing Golden Light

Now imagine a beautiful, golden, sparkling light beginning to form around your head and upper body. It can look as bright as early morning or as buttery and warming as late-afternoon sunshine. Allow this glittering, golden light to grow in size to surround you. The sparkles held within this light are the energies of everything positive: love, compassion, forgiveness, kindness, wholeness, tenderness, and every other wonderful thing you can think of.

Let the golden light continue to expand and extend outward, growing in size, flooding that space around you (your aura) with beautiful light. No physical object can interfere with this expansion—not walls, floors, objects, or other people. Your aura, six feet in all directions around you, is your very own unique and specific vibration. Allow that space to fill up with the light.

Now as you breathe in, the golden light around you is traveling on the oxygen and enters your body. The light-filled oxygen fills your lungs as you breathe.

The energy of golden light travels through your bloodstream, bringing blessings to every nook and cranny of your body, soothing you, nurturing you, and raising your vibration with every breath that you take.

Notice how you feel inside as you continue to breathe in the golden light. You are whole. You are nurtured from the inside out. The golden light is the energy of living consciousness, energy full of blessings, just for you. Allow yourself to be at peace. Envision yourself glowing and vibrant. Feel inside yourself as you breathe. Know that in this very moment, you are doing everything you can to bring glorious perfection into your life. Experience yourself as happy and peaceful.

Part Three: Reconnecting with Your Reiki Master in Spirit

Float for a moment in peace. Now use your ability to pretend, see, hear, sense, feel, or just know that you are sitting inside a huge cave, a cave so vast that you can barely make out its walls and ceiling. You find that you are sitting on soft grasses full of wildflowers in front of a bonfire with flames that are full of different colors. This is the fire of ever-flowing life. All the colors of the rainbow dance before your eyes as the flames whisper messages to you from your ancient ancestors. *You are loved. You are love. We love you. Love your Self. You are the beloved.* Sit with this for a while.

The energy all around you begins to shift; you can feel something beautiful happening. Your Reiki master in spirit appears on the other side of the bonfire, gazing at you with great respect and love. You feel safe, treasured, and so happy to be in the presence of your Reiki master in spirit as you sit with the fire of ever-flowing life between you. This is a wonderful way to develop an ever-deepening relationship with such a powerful and important guide for your life and for your healing. Your Reiki master in spirit says, *I know you wish to ask me for some things, and I say yes to you before you even ask, but please go ahead and ask me for what you want.*

You reply, *I want to find my way to my own healing.*

Yes, I will assist you.

I want to trust myself as I travel along my spiritual path.

Yes, I will help you with that.

I want to find the perfect Reiki master in my physical world with whom I can study Reiki, or from whom I could receive the greatest healing.

Yes, I will lead you to that person.

I wish to awaken to my quest and to walk my path with love and joy.

Yes, I will assist you with this.

At this point, ask anything else that is important to you personally.

Powerful light pours down from above, surrounding you and your Reiki master in spirit, washing you in beautiful divine love that activates the code within you that is your quest. Savor this and allow the light to shift your vibrations to a higher level. You can stay with this for as long as you like.

Now it is time to go back to your current life as a human on earth. You can come back here to be with your Reiki master in spirit whenever you want to. So just for now, say goodbye in whatever way feels comfortable to you.

A wind comes and blows you gently back to your human body. Feel your spirit come back inside your body. Feel your body breathing. Notice your belly and chest rising. Take your time and let yourself enjoy the sensation of being a spirit inside your body.

Welcome back!

You can always return to the cavern to be with your Reiki master in spirit whenever you wish to by repeating this meditation. But never forget: your Reiki master in spirit is with you all the time and can come to your aid in any moment in which you think of it. It is a great blessing to have a healing guide of such magnificence in your life.

Further Reading

Reiki Research and Training:

The Center for Reiki Research, Including Reiki Research in Hospitals: www.centerforreikiresearch.org

University of Minnesota, Taking Charge of Your Health: http://takingcharge.csh.umn.edu/explore-healing-practices/reiki/what-does-research-say-about-reiki

Medical Research on Reiki Therapy:

http://www.reikimedresearch.org

Raven's website:

http://ravenkeyes.com

International Center for Reiki Training (William Lee Rand): http://www.reiki.org/reikiclasses/Schedule.html#rand

The Reiki Training Program (Eileen Dey):

http://www.reikitrainingprogram.com

Books:

Cowan, Tom. *Yearning for the Wind: Celtic Reflections on Nature and the Soul.* Novato, CA: New World Library, 2003.

Ingerman, Sandra. *Soul Retrieval, Mending the Fragmented Self.* New York: Harper Collins, 1991.

Keegan, William Jr. *Closure: The Untold Story of the Ground Zero Recovery Mission.* New York: Touchstone, 2006.

Oz, Mehmet, M.D. *Healing from the Heart: How Unconventional Wisdom Unleashes the Power of Modern Medicine.* New York: Penguin, 1998.

Petter, Frank Arjava. *Reiki Fire: New Information about the Origins of the Reiki Power, A Complete Manual.* Twin Lakes, WI: Lotus Light Publications, 1997.

Pike, Signe. *Faery Tale: One Woman's Search for Enchantment in a Modern World.* New York: Penguin, 2010.

Prechtel, Martin. *Secrets of the Talking Jaguar.* New York: Putnam, 1999.

Ruiz, Don Miguel. *The Four Agreements: A Practical Guide to Personal Freedom.* San Rafael, CA: Amber-Allen Publishing, 1997.

Stein, Diane. *Essential Reiki: A Complete Guide to an Ancient Healing Art.* New York: The Crossing Press, 1995.

Music that Inspired this Book:

Michael Pestalozzi

Radiohead

Seal

Yes

Notes

1. Dee Brown, *Bury My Heart at Wounded Knee: An Indian History of the American West* (New York: Owl Books, 1970).
2. William Lee Rand, "What is the History of Reiki?" The International Center for Reiki Training, http://www.reiki.org/faq/historyofreiki.html (accessed February 2012).
3. Henry David Thoreau, *The Journal of Henry David Thoreau 1837–1861* (New York: New York Review, 2009).
4. NASA, "What is Thermodynamics?" http://www.grc.nasa.gov/WWW/k-12/airplane/thermo.html (accessed February 2012).
5. Margaret Talbot, "The Placebo Prescription," *New York Times*, January 9, 2000, http://www.nytimes.com/2000/01/09/magazine/the-placebo-prescription.

html?pagewanted=all&src=pm (accessed February 2012).

6. American Hospital Association, "Latest Survey Shows More Hospitals Offering Complementary and Alternative Medicine Services," September 15, 2008, http://www.aha.org/presscenter/pressrel/2008/080915-pr-cam.shtml (accessed February 2012).
7. William Lee Rand, "Distant Attunements," The International Center for Reiki Training, http://www.reiki.org/reikinews/Distantattunement.html (accessed February 2012).
8. Emily Dickinson, *The Complete Poems of Emily Dickinson*, ed. Thomas H. Johnson (New York: Little, Brown, 1960).
9. Mayo Clinic Staff, "Forgiveness: Letting Go of Grudges and Bitterness," Mayo Clinic blog, http://www.mayoclinic.com/health/forgiveness/MH00131 (accessed February 2012).
10. Mayo Clinic Staff, "Meditation: A Simple, Fast Way to Reduce Stress" Mayo Clinic blog, http://www.mayoclinic.com/health/meditation/HQ01070 (accessed February 2012).
11. Chip Brown, "The Experiments of Dr. Oz," *New York Times*, July 30, 1995, http://www.nytimes.com/1995/07/30/magazine/the-experiments

-of-dr-oz.html?ref=mehmetcoz (accessed February 2012).

12. Marianne Williamson, *Healing the Soul of America: Reclaiming Our Voices as Spiritual Citizens* (New York: Touchstone, 2000).
13. Good Quotes "Howard Cosell Quotes", http://www.goodquotes.com/quote/howard-cosell/sports-is-human-life-in-microcosm (accessed February 2012).
14. Oglesby Paul, *The Caring Physician: The Life of Dr. Francis W. Peabody* (Boston: Harvard University Press, 1991).
15. Sheldon Feldman, MD, FACS "Alternative Therapy for Breast Cancer: Outcomes, Obstacles and Opportunities," *Annals of Surgical Oncology* 18, no. 4 (2011).
16. Jim Gormley (FDNY), personal conversation with author, 2011.
17. Sandra Ingerman, *Soul Retrieval: Mending the Fragmented Self* (New York: Harper Collins, 1991).
18. Tom Forman and Greg Kandra, *9/11*. directed by James Hanlon, Rob Klug, Gédéon Naudet, and Jules Naudet (New York: CBS Television, 2002).
19. eMerge Military Services, http://www.emergemilitaryservices.org/Coaching.html (accessed February 2012).

20. Naomi Breslau, "Post-Traumatic Disorder, Depression Linked," Reuters, New York. http://www.hopeforhealing.org/march.html (accessed February 2012).
21. Kirsten Scharnberg, "Medicine Men for the 21st Century," *Chicago Tribune*, June 4, 2007, http://articles.chicagotribune.com/2007-06-04/news/0706030707_1_native-americans-american-indian-21st-century (accessed February 2012).
22. Eileen Dey, *Touching the World through Reiki* (Bothell, WA: Book Publishing Network, 2010).
23. Eryn Brown, "9/11 Study: Multiple Health Woes Persist for Rescue Workers," *Los Angeles Times*, September 1, 2011, http://articles.latimes.com/2011/sep/01/news/la-heb-911-illness-mental-physical-20110901 (accessed February 2012).
24. Jim Gormley (FDNY), personal conversation with author, 2011.
25. Mark Twain, *Autobiography of Mark Twain, Volume 1*, ed. Harriet E. Smith (New York: Harper Collins, 2010).
26. Margaret Bird Steinmetz, *Leaves of Life: For Daily Inspiration* (New York: Qonto, 2010).

To Write to the Author

If you wish to contact the author or would like more information about this book, please write to the author in care of Llewellyn Worldwide Ltd. and we will forward your request. Both the author and publisher appreciate hearing from you and learning of your enjoyment of this book and how it has helped you. Llewellyn Worldwide Ltd. cannot guarantee that every letter written to the author can be answered, but all will be forwarded. Please write to:

Raven Keyes
℅ Llewellyn Worldwide
2143 Wooddale Drive
Woodbury, MN 55125-2989

Please enclose a self-addressed stamped envelope for reply, or $1.00 to cover costs. If outside the U.S.A., enclose an international postal reply coupon.